CW01465134

SKIATHOS

TRAVEL GUIDE 2025

The ultimate companion for your Mediterranean adventure. From its crystal-clear waters and golden beaches to its charming villages and vibrant nightlife.

By

AARON MCCLAIN

ALL RIGHTS RESERVED

No part of this publication by Aaron McClain may be reproduced, distributed, or transmitted in any form or by any means, including photocopying, recording, or other electronic or mechanical methods, without the prior written permission of the publisher, except in the case of brief quotations embodied in critical reviews and certain other noncommercial uses permitted by copyright law.

DISCLAIMER

This travel guide is provided for informational purposes only. The information contained herein is believed to be accurate and reliable as of the publication date, but may be subject to change. We are not making any warranty, express or implied, with respect to the content of this guide.

Users of this guide are responsible for verifying information independently and consulting appropriate authorities and resources prior to travel. We are not liable for any loss or damage caused by the reliance on information contained in this guide.

Information regarding travel advisories, visas, health, safety, and other important considerations can change rapidly. Users are advised to check for the most up-to-date information from official government and travel industry sources before embarking on any trip.

Travel inherently involves risk, and users are responsible for making their own informed decisions and accepting any associated risks.

TABLE OF CONTENT

Chapter 1. Introduction

1.1 Overview of Skiathos

Nestled in the heart of the Sporades archipelago in the Aegean Sea, Skiathos is a small yet captivating island known for its lush pine forests, golden beaches, and charming Greek hospitality. Despite its compact size, measuring only 12 kilometers in length and 6 kilometers in width, the island boasts over 60 stunning beaches, including the iconic Koukounaries, often hailed as one of the best beaches in the Mediterranean.

Skiathos effortlessly blends natural beauty with cultural heritage. Its picturesque main town, Skiathos Town, features whitewashed houses with terracotta roofs, narrow cobblestone streets, and vibrant harbor scenes that reflect a quintessential Greek island charm. From exploring the 18th-century Evangelistria Monastery, where the first Greek flag was woven, to enjoying the cosmopolitan buzz of waterfront tavernas and boutique shops, visitors find a perfect balance between history and modern leisure.

The island's interior is a verdant paradise, with rolling hills covered in pine and olive trees that offer a cool respite from the sun-drenched coastline. Hikers and nature enthusiasts can explore scenic trails that lead to hidden coves, dramatic cliffs, and panoramic viewpoints.

Skiathos is not only a destination for relaxation but also a playground for adventure seekers. It offers a range of activities, from sailing and diving to windsurfing and kayaking. Additionally, it served as a filming location for the movie *Mamma Mia!*, drawing fans eager to experience its cinematic allure.

Renowned for its lively atmosphere, Skiathos welcomes travelers with an infectious energy. Its blend of natural splendor, cultural richness, and warm island spirit make it an unforgettable destination that caters to all types of travelers, whether they seek serenity, exploration, or vibrant nightlife.

1.2 History and Culture

Skiathos has a rich history that dates back to ancient times, weaving a narrative shaped by conquests, maritime trade, and cultural evolution. Archaeological evidence suggests that the island was first inhabited by Pelasgians, followed by the Chalkidians from Evia around the 8th century BCE, who established it as a prosperous maritime trading post due to its strategic location in the Aegean Sea.

During the Classical period, Skiathos aligned itself with Athens in the Delian League. The island's natural harbors and shipbuilding industry flourished, contributing to the strength of Athenian naval power. Its fortifications, including remnants of ancient walls, bear testimony to its importance in defending against pirate raids, a recurring threat throughout its history.

The island's fate changed dramatically with the rise of the Byzantine Empire, followed by Venetian and Ottoman rule. In the 14th century, the population moved from the coast to the Kastro, a fortified settlement atop a rocky promontory, to protect themselves from pirate attacks. This medieval stronghold, with its narrow alleys, battlements, and ruins of churches, remains a fascinating historical site for visitors today.

Christianity deeply influenced Skiathos' cultural heritage. The Monastery of Evangelistria, founded in 1794, played a pivotal role in the Greek War of Independence.

It is here that the first Greek flag, bearing the white cross on a blue field, was woven and blessed. The monastery remains a symbol of national pride and religious devotion.

The island's culture reflects a blend of traditional customs and modern influences. Music and dance are integral to local life, with festivals celebrating religious feast days and community events. The traditional *syrtos* and *kalamatianos* dances are performed with joy, accompanied by live folk music. Skiathos also has a literary legacy as the birthplace of Alexandros Papadiamantis, one of Greece's most esteemed writers. His house, now a museum in Skiathos Town, offers insights into his life and work, which often depict the simplicity and spirituality of island life.

Today, Skiathos seamlessly balances its historical roots with a vibrant contemporary culture. Its rich past is celebrated in museums, churches, and archaeological sites, while its cosmopolitan character shines in its cuisine, art, and hospitality. From ancient ruins to modern festivals, Skiathos offers visitors a captivating journey through time and tradition.

1.3 Why Visit Skiathos?

Skiathos is a gem in the Aegean Sea, offering a harmonious blend of breathtaking landscapes, rich history, and a lively atmosphere that appeals to all types of travelers. Here are some compelling reasons why this enchanting island should be on your travel list:

1.3.1 Stunning Beaches

With more than 60 beaches dotting its coastline, Skiathos is a paradise for beach lovers. The most famous is **Koukounaries Beach**, known for its golden sand, clear turquoise waters, and surrounding pine forest that fills the air with a refreshing scent. For those seeking seclusion, **Mandraki Beach** and **Lalaria Beach** offer dramatic landscapes and crystal-clear waters accessible by boat. Whether you prefer family-friendly shores or hidden coves, Skiathos delivers a perfect beach day for everyone.

1.3.2 Lively Island Charm

Skiathos Town is the vibrant heart of the island, filled with quaint streets, charming cafes, and stylish boutiques. Its picturesque old harbor, lined with traditional fishing boats and modern yachts, is perfect for a sunset stroll or a leisurely drink. The town's buzzing nightlife, featuring chic bars and beach clubs, attracts a cosmopolitan crowd, ensuring evenings filled with energy and fun.

1.3.3 Rich History and Culture

History enthusiasts will appreciate the island's well-preserved **Kastro**, a medieval fortress that once protected residents from pirates. A visit to the **Monastery of Evangelistria**, where the first Greek flag was raised, provides a deep connection to Greece's independence struggle. Literature fans can explore the **Alexandros Papadiamantis House-Museum**, dedicated to one of Greece's most famous authors and a native of Skiathos.

1.3.4 Outdoor Adventures

Nature lovers and adventurers will find plenty to do. The island's interior is a lush expanse of pine forests and olive groves, crisscrossed by scenic hiking trails that lead to panoramic viewpoints. Watersports enthusiasts can enjoy sailing, kayaking, and diving, while boat trips to nearby islands and hidden beaches offer a sense of exploration and discovery.

1.3.5 Accessible Yet Unspoiled

Despite its popularity, Skiathos retains a sense of authenticity and unspoiled beauty. Its airport and ferry connections make it easy to reach, but its charm lies in its balance between tourist-friendly amenities and traditional Greek island life. Visitors can enjoy luxury resorts or quaint family-run accommodations, gourmet dining or simple seaside tavernas, ensuring a personalized experience.

1.3.6 A Taste of the Cinematic

Fans of the movie *Mamma Mia!* will recognize Skiathos from its starring role alongside neighboring Skopelos. Special tours guide visitors to iconic filming locations, adding a touch of Hollywood glamour to the journey.

Skiathos combines natural splendor, cultural depth, and a festive atmosphere, making it a destination where unforgettable memories are made. Whether you're looking for relaxation, adventure, or romance, this island promises an idyllic getaway filled with sun, sea, and soul.

1.4 Best Time to Visit

The best time to visit Skiathos depends on your travel preferences, as the island offers unique experiences throughout the year. Its Mediterranean climate features hot, dry summers and mild, rainy winters, making it ideal for seasonal exploration. Here's a breakdown of what each season has to offer:

1.4.1 Summer (June to August) – Peak Season

Why Visit?
 Summer is the most popular time to visit Skiathos, attracting travelers with its sun-drenched days, warm waters, and buzzing atmosphere. Temperatures range from 25°C to 35°C (77°F to 95°F), perfect for enjoying the island's renowned beaches, vibrant nightlife, and outdoor activities.
 Highlights:

- **Beach Days:** The island's beaches, like Koukounaries and Lalaria, are in their prime.
- **Water Sports:** Sailing, windsurfing, and diving are at their best with calm seas and clear skies.
- **Festivals:** Traditional festivals and music events fill the summer nights with Greek culture.
  Considerations:
   Accommodation and flights are in high demand, so early booking is essential. Beaches and popular attractions can be crowded.

1.4.2 Spring (April to May) – A Blossoming Paradise

Why Visit?
 Spring is a fantastic time for nature lovers and hikers. The island blooms with vibrant flowers and green landscapes, and temperatures are mild, ranging from 15°C to 25°C (59°F to 77°F).
 Highlights:

- **Nature and Hiking:** Trails through pine forests and olive groves are at their most beautiful.
- **Tranquility:** Fewer tourists mean a more serene experience.
- **Lower Prices:** Flights and accommodation are more affordable than in peak season.
  Considerations:
   The sea may still be too chilly for swimming, but it's perfect for scenic boat tours.

1.4.3 Autumn (September to October) – Late Summer Magic

Why Visit?

Autumn offers the warmth of summer without the crowds. Sea temperatures remain pleasant, and the island retains its lively charm. Daytime temperatures average between 20°C and 30°C (68°F to 86°F).

Highlights:

- **Warm Waters:** The sea remains ideal for swimming well into October.
- **Harvest Season:** Enjoy fresh local produce and traditional autumn dishes.
- **Discounts:** Lower prices on accommodations and fewer tourists make travel easier.

    Considerations:
    Some tourist services may begin to wind down by mid-October.

1.4.4 Winter (November to March) – Quiet and Peaceful

Why Visit?

Winter on Skiathos is quiet and offers a glimpse into local life without the tourist crowds. It's ideal for a peaceful retreat, creative pursuits, or cultural exploration. Temperatures range from 10°C to 15°C (50°F to 59°F).

Highlights:

- **Authentic Atmosphere:** Experience the island like a local, with cozy tavernas and traditional events.
- **Exploration:** Visit historical sites, monasteries, and the old town without the rush.

    Considerations:
    Many resorts and tourist-focused businesses close for the season, and weather can be rainy.

For beach enthusiasts and nightlife seekers, **summer (June to August)** is ideal, while **spring (April to May)** and **autumn (September to October)** provide a balance of good weather, fewer crowds, and more affordable travel. **Winter** offers tranquility and cultural immersion but comes with limited tourist facilities. Choose the season that aligns with your travel style to make the most of your Skiathos adventure.

1.5 How to Use This Guide

The *Skiathos Travel Guide 2025* is designed to be your comprehensive companion, providing everything you need for a memorable visit to this enchanting Greek island. Whether you're a first-time visitor or a seasoned traveler, this guide offers practical insights, expert recommendations, and detailed itineraries to enhance your experience. Here's how to make the most of it:

1.5.1 Navigating the Chapters

Each chapter of the guide is structured to help you find information quickly and efficiently:

- **Introduction** offers an overview of Skiathos, its history, culture, and the best time to visit, helping you get a sense of the island before your trip.
- **Getting There** provides detailed travel options, including flights, ferries, and local transportation tips to help you reach and explore Skiathos with ease.
- **Top Attractions** highlights the must-see sights, from beaches and historical landmarks to nature trails and scenic viewpoints.
- **Where to Stay** and **Dining and Nightlife** sections offer tailored recommendations for every budget and preference.
- **Activities and Adventures** introduces a range of experiences, from watersports to cultural excursions, while **Shopping** showcases where to find local treasures.
- **Travel Tips** covers practical matters like currency, safety, and etiquette, ensuring a smooth trip.
- **Itineraries** are ready-made plans that cater to different travel styles and durations, simplifying your travel planning.

1.5.2 Tailoring Your Experience

Use the guide to customize your trip according to your interests:

- **Beach Lovers** will find a detailed section on the best beaches, categorized by popularity, family-friendliness, and hidden gems.
- **History Buffs** can dive into the island's cultural heritage with insights into ancient ruins, monasteries, and museums.
- **Adventure Seekers** will discover recommended hiking trails, watersports, and boat tours to fuel their wanderlust.

1.5.3 Tips for Smart Travel

- **Local Recommendations**: Look for highlighted tips from locals to uncover hidden spots and avoid tourist traps.
- **Sustainable Travel**: Embrace eco-friendly choices with suggestions on how to support local businesses and minimize your environmental footprint.
- **Seasonal Insights**: Choose your travel dates wisely with advice on the island's climate and events throughout the year.

1.5.4 On-the-Go Access

This guide is perfect for both pre-trip planning and on-the-ground reference. Use the detailed maps and itineraries to navigate Skiathos, or refer to quick tips and contact information when you need immediate answers.

By following this guide, you'll discover the magic of Skiathos while tailoring your experience to suit your preferences. Enjoy a seamless, unforgettable journey through one of Greece's most captivating islands.

Chapter 2. Getting There

2.1 By Air (Direct Flights, Connecting Flights)

Skiathos is well-connected by air, making it an easily accessible destination for travelers from across Europe and beyond. The island's **Skiathos International Airport (JSI)**, also known as **Alexandros Papadiamantis Airport**, is located just 2 kilometers from Skiathos Town, offering quick and convenient access to the island's main hub.

2.1.1 Direct Flights

During the high season (typically from May to October), several airlines operate direct flights to Skiathos from major European cities. Popular departure points include:

- **United Kingdom**: London (Heathrow, Gatwick), Manchester, and Birmingham
- **Germany**: Frankfurt, Munich, and Düsseldorf
- **Italy**: Rome and Milan
- **Netherlands**: Amsterdam
- **Austria**: Vienna

Charter and low-cost airlines like TUI, Jet2, and easyJet often provide direct seasonal services, making summer travel convenient for European tourists. For a seamless vacation, consider booking direct flights well in advance, as they fill up quickly during peak months.

2.1.2 Connecting Flights

For travelers from other parts of the world or regions without direct routes, connecting flights through Athens or Thessaloniki are common.

- **Athens International Airport (ATH)**: Olympic Air and Sky Express operate frequent domestic flights between Athens and Skiathos, with a flight time of about 45 minutes.
- **Thessaloniki Airport (SKG)**: A shorter connection from Thessaloniki takes around 30 minutes.

These connections provide flexibility for year-round travel, though schedules may be less frequent in the winter months.

2.1.3 Unique Airport Experience

Skiathos Airport is famous for its short runway and dramatic landings, offering an exhilarating experience for aviation enthusiasts. The airport's location between the sea and a lagoon makes it one of the most photographed spots in Greece, with visitors often gathering to watch planes land just meters above the road near the runway.

Tips for Air Travelers:

- **Book Early**: Direct flights are in high demand, particularly in summer.
- **Check Luggage Restrictions**: Some smaller planes may have baggage limits.
- **Arrive Early for Departures**: The airport is small, and check-in lines can be long during busy periods.

Flying to Skiathos offers breathtaking views of the Aegean and a swift start to your island adventure.

2.2 By Ferry (Ferry Routes, Schedules)

Traveling to Skiathos by ferry is a scenic and popular option, especially for those exploring multiple Greek islands or starting their journey from mainland Greece. The island is part of the Sporades archipelago, making it accessible via regular ferry services from key ports.

2.2.1 Ferry Routes to Skiathos

Ferries to Skiathos connect from several mainland ports and neighboring islands:

- **From Volos**:
  Volos is the primary port for reaching Skiathos, offering year-round ferry service. High-speed catamarans operated by **Blue Star Ferries**, **ANES Ferries**, and **Seajets** take approximately 2 to 2.5 hours, while conventional ferries take about 3.5 hours.

    - **High-Speed Ferries**: Faster but more expensive.
    - **Conventional Ferries**: Ideal for travelers with vehicles or large luggage.
- **From Agios Konstantinos**:
  Agios Konstantinos, located about 165 km north of Athens, provides seasonal ferry services to Skiathos. Ferries are operated by **Anes Ferries** with a travel time of around 2 to 3 hours.

- **From Mantoudi (Evia Island)**:
  Mantoudi offers another route to Skiathos, especially popular with travelers coming from Athens or central Greece. Ferries operated by **Anes Ferries** take approximately 1.5 to 2 hours, depending on the type of vessel.

- **From Thessaloniki** (Summer only):
  Seasonal ferries connect Thessaloniki with Skiathos in summer, providing a direct link from northern Greece. The journey takes approximately 3.5 to 4 hours, operated by **Blue Star Ferries** or **Seajets**.

- **From Neighboring Sporades Islands (Skopelos, Alonissos)**:
  Short ferry rides connect Skiathos with **Skopelos** and **Alonissos**, making island-hopping convenient. These routes are frequently served by **Seajets** and **ANES Ferries**, with travel times ranging from 30 minutes to 1 hour.

2.2.2 Ferry Schedules

- **High Season (June to September)**: Ferries operate multiple times a day, with more frequent departures in July and August.
- **Off-Season (October to May)**: Fewer ferry options are available, and schedules are less predictable. Weather conditions may affect service in winter months.

2.2.3 Booking and Tips

- **Advance Booking**: For summer travel, book tickets early, especially for high-speed ferries.
- **Seating Options**: Choose between economy, business, or VIP classes on larger vessels.
- **Vehicle Transport**: If bringing a car or motorcycle, confirm availability as space is limited on many routes.
- **Weather Considerations**: High winds can disrupt ferry schedules; plan for possible delays.

Ferry travel to Skiathos provides a relaxing and picturesque approach, with panoramic sea views and the excitement of arriving at a classic Greek island port. It's an experience that complements the island's charm and adds a touch of adventure to your journey.

2.3 By Private Yacht or Boat

For those seeking a personalized and luxurious journey, arriving in Skiathos by private yacht or boat is an exceptional way to experience the island's captivating coastline and turquoise waters. With its well-equipped marinas, scenic anchorages, and a strategic position in the Sporades archipelago, Skiathos is a favored destination for sailors and yachting enthusiasts.

2.3.1 Ports and Marinas

- **Skiathos Port (Main Harbor)**: Located in Skiathos Town, this bustling harbor is the primary docking point for yachts and boats. It offers mooring for vessels of various sizes and provides essential services such as water, electricity, and refueling facilities. The port's central location allows easy access to shops, tavernas, and the vibrant nightlife of Skiathos Town.
- **New Marina Skiathos**: Adjacent to the main harbor, this recently developed marina offers modern amenities and improved docking space, catering to larger yachts. It's ideal for longer stays and those requiring full marine services.
- **Koukounaries Bay**: While not a marina, this famous beach offers a picturesque anchorage with calm waters and a stunning backdrop of pine forests. It's perfect for a day stop or a leisurely swim.

2.3.2 Sailing Routes to Skiathos

Skiathos is easily accessible from mainland Greece and nearby islands:

- **From Volos or Evia**: These routes are popular for private boat charters and offer scenic cruising through the Sporades archipelago.
- **Island-Hopping in the Sporades**: Sail from **Skopelos**, **Alonissos**, and **Skyros**, exploring each island's unique charm before docking in Skiathos.

2.3.3 Entry Requirements and Formalities

- **Customs and Immigration**: If arriving from outside Greece, ensure compliance with Greek maritime entry regulations. Have passports, registration, and insurance documents ready for inspection.
- **Mooring Permits**: Obtain mooring permits where necessary, particularly during the peak summer season. Early reservations are recommended for marina space.

2.3.4 Sailing Tips

- **Weather Conditions**: The Aegean Sea is known for the **Meltemi winds**, particularly in July and August. These strong northern winds can affect navigation, so monitor forecasts and plan routes carefully.
- **Anchorages**: The southern coast of Skiathos offers sheltered bays and calm waters, while the northern coast is more exposed. Popular anchoring spots include **Kanapitsa Bay** and **Megali Ammos Beach**.
- **Supplies and Refueling**: Skiathos Town has well-stocked supply stores and fuel stations. Provisioning can be done easily before setting off to explore more remote areas.

2.3.5 Chartering a Boat

If you don't own a yacht but want to experience the luxury of sailing around Skiathos, boat charter services are widely available. Options range from bareboat charters for experienced sailors to fully crewed yachts for a premium experience.

Sailing to Skiathos offers unparalleled freedom and a chance to discover hidden coves, unspoiled beaches, and crystal-clear waters at your own pace. It's a journey that embodies the essence of Greek island life—adventurous, serene, and filled with stunning natural beauty.

2.4 Transportation on the Island (Taxis, Buses, Car Rentals)

Getting around Skiathos is straightforward, with a variety of transportation options to suit different travel styles. Whether you prefer the convenience of taxis, the affordability of buses, or the flexibility of a rental car or scooter, the island's compact size makes travel efficient and enjoyable.

2.4.1 Taxis

Taxis are a convenient way to travel across Skiathos, especially for quick trips or when public transport is unavailable.

- **Taxi Ranks**: The main taxi stand is located in **Skiathos Town**, near the harbor. Taxis can also be found at **Skiathos International Airport (JSI)** and popular beaches like Koukounaries.
- **Booking a Taxi**: You can flag down a taxi on the street, call for one, or use mobile apps that support local services.
- **Fares**: Taxi fares are metered but can vary depending on distance, time of day, and luggage. Confirm prices for longer trips, such as to remote beaches or inland villages.
- **Shared Rides**: Sharing taxis with other travelers heading in the same direction is common and can reduce costs.

2.4.2 Buses

The bus system in Skiathos is efficient, affordable, and widely used by both locals and tourists.

- **Main Bus Route**: A single primary bus line runs from **Skiathos Town** to **Koukounaries Beach**, stopping at major points along the southern coast.
- **Stops and Frequency**:

- There are 26 marked stops along the route, serving popular destinations like **Megali Ammos**, **Agia Paraskevi**, and **Troulos**.
- During summer, buses run frequently (every 10 to 20 minutes). In the off-season, service is less frequent.
- **Tickets and Fares**:
  - Purchase tickets directly from the driver or at kiosks in Skiathos Town.
  - Fares are affordable, with prices depending on the distance traveled.

Tips:

- Buses can be crowded in peak season, so arrive early to secure a seat, especially for trips to popular beaches.
- Pay attention to the bus schedule for the last return trip to avoid being stranded.

2.4.3 Car and Scooter Rentals

Renting a car, scooter, or ATV provides the most flexibility for exploring Skiathos at your own pace.

- **Rental Agencies**: Numerous agencies operate in Skiathos Town and near the airport. Reputable local and international providers offer a range of vehicles.
- **Car Rentals**:
  - Ideal for reaching remote beaches and exploring inland areas.
  - **Driving Requirements**: A valid driver's license (an International Driving Permit may be required for non-EU visitors).
  - **Road Conditions**: Main roads are paved and well-maintained, but some beaches, like Lalaria, require a boat trip due to challenging access.
- **Scooter and ATV Rentals**:
  - Scooters are perfect for solo travelers or couples and are easy to park.
  - ATVs offer a fun alternative for adventurous routes and sandy paths.
  - Helmets are mandatory, and rental agencies usually provide them.

Tips for Renting:

- **Book Early**: Vehicles can sell out quickly in the summer season.
- **Insurance**: Ensure your rental includes comprehensive insurance.
- **Fuel**: Gas stations are limited outside Skiathos Town; refuel before venturing far.

2.4.4 Bicycle Rentals

For eco-friendly travel, bicycles are available for rent in Skiathos Town. Cycling is ideal for short distances or exploring flat coastal routes, though the island's hilly terrain may challenge some riders.

- **Taxis** are best for convenience and short trips.
- **Buses** offer a reliable and economical option for beach-hopping along the southern coast.
- **Car, scooter, or ATV rentals** give you freedom to explore hidden gems off the main route.
- **Bicycles** provide a scenic and sustainable travel alternative.

Choosing the right transportation method will enhance your Skiathos adventure, making it easy to uncover the island's beauty and charm.

Chapter 3. Accommodation

3.1 Luxury Hotels and Resorts

Skiathos offers a range of luxury accommodations that provide premium comfort, stunning views, and world-class services. Below are detailed options for discerning travelers seeking elegance and exclusivity.

1. Elivi Skiathos

- **Price Range**: €300 – €1,000+ per night, depending on the season and room type
- **Address**: Koukounaries Bay, 37002 Skiathos, Greece
- **Contact**: +30 24274 40950
- **Website**: elivihotels.com
- **Location**: Overlooking the famous Koukounaries Beach, surrounded by a lush pine forest
- **Key Features**:
    - Private villas and rooms with sea or forest views
    - Private pools, outdoor infinity pools, and direct beach access
    - Multiple gourmet dining options, including fine Mediterranean cuisine
    - Elivi Spa offering wellness treatments and therapies
    - Fitness center, yoga classes, and tennis courts
- **Visitor Services**:
    - Personalized concierge service
    - Luxury airport transfer
    - Beachside cabanas with butler service
    - Complimentary high-speed Wi-Fi

2. Skiathos Princess Resort

- **Price Range**: €250 – €800+ per night
- **Address**: Agia Paraskevi, 37002 Skiathos, Greece
- **Contact**: +30 24270 49731
- **Website**: skiathosprincess.com
- **Location**: Directly on the sandy beach of Agia Paraskevi, ideal for family stays
- **Key Features**:
    - Spacious rooms and suites with private terraces
    - Outdoor pool and children's pool
    - Award-winning **Harmony Spa** with natural therapies
    - Gourmet dining at multiple restaurants, including poolside options

- **Visitor Services**:
  - Kids' club and babysitting services
  - Water sports center with equipment rentals
  - Shuttle services to Skiathos Town

3. Atrium Hotel

- **Price Range**: €180 – €500+ per night
- **Address**: Agia Paraskevi, 37002 Skiathos, Greece
- **Contact**: +30 24270 49320
- **Website**: atriumhotel.gr
- **Location**: Hillside with panoramic views of Agia Paraskevi Beach
- **Key Features**:
  - Elegantly designed rooms with handcrafted furniture
  - Rooftop infinity pool with stunning sea views
  - Fitness room and sauna
  - Mediterranean cuisine at the **Atrium Restaurant**
- **Visitor Services**:
  - Free shuttle to nearby beaches
  - Concierge for private excursions
  - Car and yacht rental assistance

4. Kassandra Bay Resort & Spa

- **Price Range**: €220 – €750+ per night
- **Address**: Vassilias Beach, 37002 Skiathos, Greece
- **Contact**: +30 24270 23101
- **Website**: kassandrabay.com
- **Location**: On Vassilias Beach, 3 km from Skiathos Town
- **Key Features**:
  - Suites and villas with private pools
  - Private beach area with sunbeds
  - Two outdoor swimming pools and a heated indoor pool
  - Full-service **Kassandra Bay Spa**
- **Visitor Services**:
  - Exclusive dining experiences
  - Private boat rentals
  - Babysitting and family-friendly amenities

These luxury options in Skiathos offer unparalleled experiences, blending Greek hospitality with top-notch amenities. Prices vary seasonally, so booking early ensures the best rates.

3.2 Mid-Range Hotels

For travelers seeking comfort and quality without the premium price tag, Skiathos offers a wide range of mid-range hotels that offer great value. These accommodations provide excellent amenities, ideal for both couples and families, and are often located near popular beaches and the town center.

1. Hotel Skiathos Palace

- **Price Range**: €120 – €300+ per night
- **Address**: Koukounaries, 37002 Skiathos, Greece
- **Contact**: +30 24274 07000
- **Website**: skiathos-palace.gr
- **Location**: Nestled on the hillside of Koukounaries, overlooking the stunning Koukounaries Beach
- **Key Features**:
  - Classic rooms and suites with beautiful sea views
  - Large outdoor swimming pool and poolside bar
  - On-site restaurant serving Mediterranean and Greek cuisine
  - Close proximity to the famous Koukounaries Beach
- **Visitor Services**:
  - Free shuttle service to Skiathos Town
  - 24-hour reception and concierge
  - Daily housekeeping and room service
  - Car and bike rentals available

2. Bourtzi Hotel

- **Price Range**: €100 – €250+ per night
- **Address**: 37002 Skiathos, Greece
- **Contact**: +30 24270 22888
- **Website**: bourtzihotel.gr
- **Location**: Located in Skiathos Town, close to the harbor and local attractions
- **Key Features**:
  - Modern rooms with city or sea views
  - Outdoor pool with lounge area and sunbeds
  - Beautifully landscaped garden

- A short walk from the lively center of Skiathos Town and its vibrant nightlife
- **Visitor Services**:
  - Free Wi-Fi in all areas
  - 24-hour reception and concierge service
  - Bar and café for casual dining
  - Laundry and ironing services available

3. Paradise Hotel

- **Price Range**: €80 – €230+ per night
- **Address**: Agia Paraskevi, 37002 Skiathos, Greece
- **Contact**: +30 24270 49392
- **Website**: paradisehotel.gr
- **Location**: Set in a tranquil area near Agia Paraskevi Beach, ideal for a peaceful stay
- **Key Features**:
  - Spacious rooms with private balconies overlooking the garden or the sea
  - Traditional Greek style with modern amenities
  - Outdoor pool with a sunbathing terrace
  - Full-service restaurant offering Greek and international dishes
- **Visitor Services**:
  - Free parking and shuttle services to the beach
  - Tour desk with booking services for excursions
  - Daily cleaning and room service
  - Car and scooter rentals on-site

4. Aegean Suites Hotel

- **Price Range**: €150 – €350+ per night
- **Address**: Vassilias Beach, 37002 Skiathos, Greece
- **Contact**: +30 24270 27170
- **Website**: aegeansuites.com
- **Location**: Located on the beautiful Vassilias Beach, only a few minutes from Skiathos Town
- **Key Features**:
  - Stylish suites with luxurious amenities, most with sea views
  - Exclusive beach access with a private section of the beach
  - Private outdoor pool for suites, in addition to the main hotel pool
  - Full-service restaurant offering Greek and Mediterranean specialties

- **Visitor Services**:
  - Private yacht and boat charter services
  - Concierge service for tailored experiences
  - Fitness center and wellness treatments available
  - Transfers to Skiathos Town and the airport

5. Villa Mercedes

- **Price Range**: €100 – €270+ per night
- **Address**: 37002 Skiathos, Greece
- **Contact**: +30 24270 23537
- **Website**: villamercedes.gr
- **Location**: Near the center of Skiathos Town, offering easy access to shops, restaurants, and beaches
- **Key Features**:
  - Comfortable, well-equipped rooms with sea or town views
  - Relaxing outdoor pool area surrounded by gardens
  - Traditional Greek-style décor with modern comforts
  - Family-friendly accommodations with connecting rooms
- **Visitor Services**:
  - Free Wi-Fi in all rooms and public areas
  - Car and motorbike rentals available
  - 24-hour front desk with tour booking assistance
  - On-site bar and café for light meals and drinks

These mid-range hotels in Skiathos offer the perfect balance of affordability and quality, providing guests with everything needed for a comfortable and memorable stay. With excellent locations near popular beaches and Skiathos Town, they allow easy access to the island's best attractions while offering a relaxed atmosphere. Be sure to book in advance, particularly during the busy summer season.

3.3 Budget-Friendly Options

Skiathos offers several affordable accommodations that provide excellent value for money without compromising on comfort or convenience. These budget-friendly options cater to travelers who want to enjoy the beauty of the island while keeping costs low.

1. Hotel Christina

- **Price Range**: €50 – €150+ per night
- **Address**: Skiathos Town, 37002 Skiathos, Greece

- **Contact**: +30 24270 24991
- **Website**: hotelchristina.gr
- **Location**: Centrally located in Skiathos Town, just a short walk from the harbor and local attractions
- **Key Features**:
  - Simple, well-maintained rooms with private balconies
  - Family-run hotel with a welcoming atmosphere
  - Close proximity to shops, restaurants, and the nightlife of Skiathos Town
  - Easy access to the bus station for exploring the island
- **Visitor Services**:
  - 24-hour reception with friendly staff to assist with tours and recommendations
  - Free Wi-Fi in all areas
  - Continental breakfast served daily
  - Daily cleaning and room service

2. Hotel Margarita

- **Price Range**: €60 – €140+ per night
- **Address**: Skiathos Town, 37002 Skiathos, Greece
- **Contact**: +30 24270 23995
- **Website**: hotelmargarita.gr
- **Location**: Situated in the heart of Skiathos Town, a few minutes' walk from the harbor
- **Key Features**:
  - Basic yet comfortable rooms with a charming local vibe
  - Ideal for those who want to explore the island without the luxury price tag
  - Balcony or terrace with most rooms, some offering scenic views of the town
  - A small garden area to relax in
- **Visitor Services**:
  - Free Wi-Fi throughout the hotel
  - Complimentary breakfast each morning
  - Car rental services available at the front desk
  - Daily housekeeping

3. Pension Margarita

- **Price Range**: €50 – €120+ per night
- **Address**: Skiathos Town, 37002 Skiathos, Greece
- **Contact**: +30 24270 22385

- **Website**: pensionmargarita.gr
- **Location**: A 10-minute walk from the heart of Skiathos Town, offering a quiet escape close to the action
- **Key Features**:
  - Affordable rooms with a homely atmosphere
  - Simple furnishings with all the essentials for a comfortable stay
  - Close to the main bus stop, making it easy to access beaches and attractions
- **Visitor Services**:
  - Free Wi-Fi in common areas and rooms
  - Airport shuttle services on request
  - Laundry services available
  - Local tours and excursions can be booked through the reception

4. Vasso's Studios

- **Price Range**: €40 – €100+ per night
- **Address**: Skiathos Town, 37002 Skiathos, Greece
- **Contact**: +30 24270 23972
- **Website**: vassosstudios.gr
- **Location**: Centrally located in Skiathos Town, with easy access to the harbor and bus station
- **Key Features**:
  - Affordable, self-catering studios ideal for independent travelers
  - Fully equipped kitchenettes, perfect for longer stays or those who prefer to cook
  - Clean and comfortable rooms with simple, functional furnishings
- **Visitor Services**:
  - Free Wi-Fi available in all rooms
  - Daily cleaning service
  - Assistance with car and scooter rentals
  - Laundry facilities available on-site

5. Aegean Hotel

- **Price Range**: €55 – €130+ per night
- **Address**: Skiathos Town, 37002 Skiathos, Greece
- **Contact**: +30 24270 22642
- **Website**: aegeanhotel.gr
- **Location**: Located in Skiathos Town, near the harbor and the island's lively nightlife scene

- **Key Features**:
  - Simple, comfortable rooms with modern amenities
  - Most rooms offer views of Skiathos Town or the harbor
  - Ideal for travelers looking for affordable accommodations with easy access to the town's amenities
- **Visitor Services**:
  - Free Wi-Fi throughout the property
  - 24-hour reception desk
  - Breakfast available upon request
  - Car and bike rental options

These budget-friendly accommodations in Skiathos provide a variety of choices for travelers who want to enjoy the island's beauty without breaking the bank. Each property offers essential services and is strategically located for easy access to beaches, shops, and the vibrant local culture. With clean, simple, and comfortable options, these hotels and studios allow guests to focus on experiencing the charm of Skiathos while enjoying affordable stays.

3.4 Villas and Unique Stays

For those seeking more privacy, space, and a distinct experience on Skiathos, villas and unique stays offer a perfect blend of comfort and luxury. These properties allow guests to immerse themselves in the island's natural beauty, often with stunning views, private pools, and access to some of the island's most serene spots.

1. Skiathos Luxury Villas

- **Price Range**: €250 – €1,000+ per night
- **Address**: Koukounaries, 37002 Skiathos, Greece
- **Contact**: +30 24270 40700
- **Website**: skiathosluxuryvillas.gr
- **Location**: Located in the Koukounaries area, known for its stunning beaches and lush surroundings
- **Key Features**:
  - Exclusive private villas with multiple bedrooms, ideal for families or groups
  - Panoramic views of the Aegean Sea and nearby beaches
  - Large private swimming pools, spacious gardens, and outdoor dining areas
  - Fully equipped kitchens, offering guests the flexibility to prepare meals
  - Contemporary, high-end furnishings and luxury bathrooms

- **Visitor Services**:
  - 24/7 concierge service for arranging excursions, transfers, and special requests
  - Daily housekeeping and cleaning service
  - Grocery delivery service available for self-catering options
  - Private chef service upon request
  - Luxury transportation options including private yachts or helicopter transfers

2. Villa Aegean

- **Price Range**: €200 – €600+ per night
- **Address**: Vassilias, 37002 Skiathos, Greece
- **Contact**: +30 24270 27287
- **Website**: villa-aegean.gr
- **Location**: Situated in a secluded hillside location, offering breathtaking views over the Aegean Sea
- **Key Features**:
  - Elegant villa with 3–4 bedrooms, ideal for families or small groups
  - Private infinity pool with sweeping sea views
  - Spacious outdoor terrace with dining area and BBQ facilities
  - Fully equipped kitchen, comfortable living spaces, and modern décor
  - Proximity to both Vassilias Beach and Skiathos Town
- **Visitor Services**:
  - Airport transfers and private chauffeur service
  - Concierge available for booking activities such as boat trips and excursions
  - Housekeeping and change of linens on request
  - Car and scooter rentals available
  - In-villa dining options from local chefs

3. Agia Paraskevi Villas

- **Price Range**: €150 – €500+ per night
- **Address**: Agia Paraskevi, 37002 Skiathos, Greece
- **Contact**: +30 24270 49153
- **Website**: agiamvillas.gr
- **Location**: Located near the peaceful Agia Paraskevi Beach, offering tranquil surroundings
- **Key Features**:
  - Traditional Greek-style villas with modern amenities and rustic charm
  - Spacious, private gardens and outdoor pools

- Some villas feature hot tubs, while others offer panoramic sea views
- Walking distance to the beach, making it ideal for those looking for a beachside retreat
- **Visitor Services**:
  - Personalized concierge service for tailored experiences and booking local activities
  - Daily cleaning service and change of linens
  - Breakfast delivery service available
  - Car and boat rentals for exploring the island

4. Skiathos Blue Villas

- **Price Range**: €180 – €450+ per night
- **Address**: Skiathos Town, 37002 Skiathos, Greece
- **Contact**: +30 24270 22050
- **Website**: skiathosbluevillas.gr
- **Location**: A hillside location offering panoramic views of Skiathos Town and the surrounding islands
- **Key Features**:
  - Stylish, contemporary villas with one to three bedrooms
  - Private infinity pools with unobstructed views of the Aegean Sea
  - Fully furnished with modern kitchens, spacious living areas, and comfortable bedrooms
  - Perfect for couples, families, or small groups looking for a peaceful, private getaway
- **Visitor Services**:
  - 24-hour concierge service for custom-tailored excursions, such as private yacht charters
  - Maid service and daily cleaning
  - Complimentary Wi-Fi and satellite TV
  - Transfer services from the airport or port
  - Grocery shopping and meal delivery upon request

5. Villa Akropolis

- **Price Range**: €170 – €450+ per night
- **Address**: Troulos, 37002 Skiathos, Greece
- **Contact**: +30 24270 49455
- **Website**: villakropolis.gr
- **Location**: Located in the tranquil area of Troulos, surrounded by pine trees and close to beautiful beaches

- **Key Features**:
  - Spacious 3-bedroom villa with modern architecture and stunning outdoor spaces
  - Private swimming pool with sunbeds and shaded terrace
  - Fully equipped kitchen, dining area, and BBQ facilities for guests' convenience
  - Ideal for families or groups seeking a private retreat with easy access to local attractions
- **Visitor Services**:
  - Concierge services for arranging excursions, activities, and restaurant bookings
  - Private airport transfers and car rental assistance
  - Daily maid service
  - Beach equipment such as umbrellas and towels available for use

These villas and unique stays offer unparalleled privacy and comfort, perfect for those seeking a more personalized experience on Skiathos. Whether you're looking for a modern villa with a private pool or a traditional Greek-style stay with stunning sea views, these properties provide an exclusive escape while still being close to the island's best attractions. With services such as concierge, private chefs, and tailored excursions, guests can enjoy a luxury experience tailored to their every need.

3.5 Booking Tips and Recommendations

Booking accommodation on Skiathos requires a bit of planning, especially during peak seasons. To ensure a seamless experience, here are some essential tips and recommendations for making the most of your stay on the island. This section will also include a few notable booking platforms and agencies that can help you find the best deals and options.

1. Book Early, Especially During Peak Season

- **Why**: Skiathos is a popular destination, particularly in the summer months (June to September). Booking early ensures you get the accommodation you desire, whether it's a luxury hotel, budget option, or private villa. This is particularly important for high-demand areas like Koukounaries Beach or Skiathos Town.
- **Price Range**: Booking early can sometimes secure discounts, with prices ranging from €50 per night for budget stays to €1,000+ per night for luxury villas during peak season.

- **Recommendation**:
  - **Website**: Booking.com, Airbnb, and Expedia offer competitive rates and a variety of options for all budgets.

2. Consider Renting a Car or Scooter for Flexibility

- **Why**: Skiathos is a small island, but some accommodations are located in more remote areas or on hillsides. Renting a car or scooter gives you the flexibility to explore more beaches, towns, and attractions.
- **Price Range**:
  - **Car Rentals**: €30 – €80 per day
  - **Scooter Rentals**: €15 – €30 per day
- **Key Features**:
  - Many accommodations offer deals with local rental agencies.
  - Vehicles are available at most major hotels, guesthouses, and at the Skiathos airport.
  - Pre-booking is recommended, especially during the peak season.
- **Recommendation**:
  - **Car and Scooter Rentals**: Skiathos Rent a Car, Skiathos Cars, and Skiathos Bikes

3. Choose Accommodation Close to Public Transport or Major Attractions

- **Why**: If you plan on exploring the island without a rental car, consider booking a place near Skiathos Town or bus stops. The island's bus system is efficient, and there are direct routes to popular beaches like Koukounaries and Banana Beach.
- **Price Range**:
  - Budget hotels or guesthouses in or near Skiathos Town: €50 – €150 per night
  - Mid-range hotels with convenient access to transport: €100 – €250 per night
- **Key Features**:
  - Proximity to bus stations, which connect major beaches and attractions.
  - Easy access to local markets, restaurants, and bars.
- **Recommendation**:
  - **Location Suggestions**: Skiathos Town, Platanias, or the beaches close to the bus routes (e.g., Koukounaries, Agia Paraskevi).
  - **Public Transportation Information**: Visit Skiathos Bus Service for timetables and routes.

4. Use Trusted Booking Websites for Transparency and Reviews

- **Why**: When booking accommodation, it's important to use reputable websites that provide clear pricing, guest reviews, and real-time availability. Reviews offer insights into the quality and service of the property.
- **Price Range**: Prices vary widely based on the platform and the property, but booking through these sites often ensures reliable service.
- **Key Features**:
  - Verified guest reviews
  - Transparent pricing with no hidden fees
  - Ability to filter options based on your preferences (e.g., location, amenities, guest rating)
- **Recommendation**:
  - **Website Suggestions**: Booking.com, Agoda, and Trivago

5. Check Cancellation Policies

- **Why**: In case your travel plans change, it's important to ensure that your accommodation offers flexible cancellation policies. Some properties may allow free cancellation up to a certain period before your stay, while others might charge a fee.
- **Price Range**: No additional charges for flexible cancellation (if booked with certain policies). Non-refundable rates may offer discounts.
- **Key Features**:
  - Flexible booking options can give peace of mind, especially during uncertain times.
  - Non-refundable options may provide discounts, but always check the cancellation policy before booking.
- **Recommendation**:
  - Look for properties labeled "Free Cancellation" or check the terms before completing your reservation.

6. Consider Staying in Alternative Locations for Lower Prices

- **Why**: While Skiathos Town and the famous beaches like Koukounaries are popular, you can often find better deals in quieter areas or in the countryside. These locations still offer easy access to the main attractions and provide a more relaxed, peaceful atmosphere.
- **Price Range**:
  - Alternative locations: €50 – €150 per night (budget to mid-range)
  - More remote areas or village stays: €60 – €200 per night

- **Key Features**:
  - Quieter, more serene areas away from the crowds
  - Often less expensive while still offering quality services
  - Access to local villages with authentic Greek experiences
- **Recommendation**:
  - **Location Suggestions**: Agia Paraskevi, Troulos, or Vassilias
  - **Booking Platforms**: Airbnb, HomeAway, and Vrbo

7. Look for Package Deals (Accommodation + Activities)

- **Why**: Package deals can offer significant savings, especially if you are planning activities such as boat tours, excursions, or rental services. Many booking platforms or local agencies offer packages that combine accommodation with popular activities.
- **Price Range**:
  - Package deals can range from €200 – €500 per person, depending on the activities included (e.g., tours, private yachts, guided trips).
- **Key Features**:
  - Combine your accommodation with local tours or experiences (e.g., boat excursions, guided hiking trips).
  - Enjoy discounts when booking activities in advance with your stay.
- **Recommendation**:
  - **Package Websites**: Viator, GetYourGuide, and Skiathos Tours

These booking tips and recommendations can help you secure the best accommodation for your stay in Skiathos while ensuring you get the most value for your budget. Remember to plan ahead, especially during the summer months, and consider various booking platforms for the best rates and options tailored to your needs. Whether you're looking for a central location in Skiathos Town or a peaceful retreat near secluded beaches, the right planning can make all the difference in ensuring a memorable holiday.

Chapter 4. Top Attractions

4.1 Skiathos Town (Old Town, Port, Main Streets)

Skiathos Town, also known as Chora, is the bustling capital of the island, filled with historical charm, vibrant street life, and stunning views of the Aegean Sea. Whether you're wandering through its cobbled streets, enjoying the lively atmosphere of the port, or exploring the main streets filled with shops, restaurants, and cafes, Skiathos Town offers a rich experience for all visitors. Here's a detailed look at the top attractions within Skiathos Town.

1. Old Town (Chora)

- **Location**: The Old Town is the heart of Skiathos Town, just a short walk from the port.
- **Price**: Free to explore; some sites may charge a small entry fee (e.g., museums).
- **Opening Hours**: Open year-round; specific attractions like museums and churches have their own schedules.
- **Website**: No official website, but general info can be found on Skiathos Island official tourism site.
- **Key Features**:
  - Traditional Greek architecture with narrow, winding streets.
  - Quaint whitewashed houses adorned with colorful flowers, particularly bougainvillea.
  - A blend of local shops, cafes, tavernas, and art galleries.
- **Visitor Services**: Tourist information stands are available around the town, providing maps and details on nearby attractions. Several guided walking tours are available to explore the Old Town.
- **Description**: Skiathos Old Town is a beautiful maze of cobbled streets and alleys, offering an authentic Greek island experience. Here, visitors can enjoy traditional tavernas offering fresh seafood, boutique shops, and local art galleries. The town retains a lot of its old-world charm, with Venetian-style buildings and panoramic views of the Aegean Sea.

2. Port of Skiathos

- **Location**: The port is located at the center of Skiathos Town, accessible from the Old Town and main streets.
- **Price**: Free to explore; cost for dining or activities along the port varies.
- **Opening Hours**: Open year-round; the restaurants and cafes along the port have varying opening hours, typically from morning to late evening.
- **Website**: No specific website for the port itself. For ferry schedules and updates, visit Skiathos Port Authority.
- **Key Features**:
  - A bustling waterfront with luxury yachts, fishing boats, and ferries.
  - Numerous waterfront cafes, bars, and restaurants offering fresh seafood and local Greek cuisine.
  - Spectacular views of the harbor, nearby islands, and Aegean waters.
- **Visitor Services**:
  - Ferry services to other islands in the Sporades and mainland Greece.
  - Tourist shops and rental agencies near the port.
  - Boat trips and day cruises departing from the port, including private yacht rentals and group tours.
- **Description**: The Port of Skiathos is one of the island's busiest spots, with ferries constantly coming and going. It's the gateway to the island, offering visitors a first glimpse of the island's stunning landscape. Whether you're arriving by ferry or simply taking a stroll along the promenade, the port area is perfect for dining and enjoying the bustling atmosphere.

3. Papadiamantis Street

- **Location**: Papadiamantis Street runs through the heart of Skiathos Town and is one of the most iconic streets on the island.
- **Price**: Free to explore; cost depends on purchases from shops, cafes, and restaurants.
- **Opening Hours**: Shops typically open from 9:00 AM – 1:00 PM and 5:00 PM – 9:00 PM. Restaurants and cafes are open all day, usually from 8:00 AM – late evening.
- **Website**: No official website for the street, but local tourism sites provide information on events and festivals.
- **Key Features**:
  - Lined with boutiques, art galleries, and souvenir shops.
  - Bustling pedestrian-friendly thoroughfare perfect for leisurely walks.
  - Named after Alexandros Papadiamantis, one of Greece's most famous writers.
- **Visitor Services**:
  - Tourist information kiosks near the street.
  - Shops offering maps, local crafts, and books related to Papadiamantis.
  - Local tour guides offer walking tours that take you along Papadiamantis Street to explore the writer's life and work.
- **Description**: Papadiamantis Street is the main artery of Skiathos Town and is known for its lively atmosphere. Named after the famous Greek writer, this street is filled with colorful boutiques, cafes, and art galleries. It's the ideal place to shop for unique souvenirs, enjoy a coffee, and experience the vibrant pulse of the town.

4. Bourtzi Peninsula

- **Location**: At the entrance of Skiathos Port, accessible by foot from the Old Town or the port.
- **Price**: Free to explore; the nearby cafe may charge for drinks.
- **Opening Hours**: Open year-round. The café operates from 10:00 AM – 7:00 PM.
- **Website**: No official website; information is available through local tourism sites.
- **Key Features**:
  - Venetian fortress ruins with sweeping views of Skiathos Town and the Aegean Sea.
  - A tranquil green space perfect for picnics, strolls, and scenic views.
  - A small café offering drinks and snacks with an incredible view of the harbor.

- **Visitor Services**:
  - Walking paths and signs detailing the history of the site.
  - A café for refreshments while enjoying the stunning views.
- **Description**: The Bourtzi Peninsula is a historical landmark located at the entrance to Skiathos Town's harbor. The area features the ruins of a Venetian fortress that once protected the island from pirates. Visitors can wander through the remains of the fortress while enjoying panoramic views of the town and the sea. It's a peaceful escape from the hustle and bustle of the town.

5. Skiathos Castle (Kastro)

- **Location**: Located about 7 km northeast of Skiathos Town, on the island's north coast.
- **Price**: Free to visit.
- **Opening Hours**: Open daily from 9:00 AM – 7:00 PM.
- **Website**: No specific website.
- **Key Features**:
  - A 13th-century Venetian castle offering breathtaking views of the island and surrounding waters.
  - Historical site with remnants of the medieval castle and church ruins.
  - Remote location with a 15-minute walk to the top.
- **Visitor Services**:
  - Information signs explaining the history of the castle.
  - The hike to the castle is relatively easy but requires good footwear.
- **Description**: Skiathos Castle is one of the island's most significant historical sites. Built in the 13th century, this medieval castle is perched on a hilltop offering panoramic views of Skiathos and neighboring islands. Although the

castle itself is in ruins, its historical significance and the view make it an essential stop for history buffs and those seeking scenic views of the island.

6. The Church of Agios Nikolaos

- **Location**: Situated in the center of Skiathos Town, near the main square.
- **Price**: Free entry.
- **Opening Hours**: Open daily from 8:00 AM – 1:00 PM and 5:00 PM – 8:00 PM.
- **Website**: No official website.
- **Key Features**:
  - Beautiful 19th-century church with intricate iconography and a peaceful courtyard.
  - Home to some of the finest examples of Byzantine religious art in Greece.
  - Regular services and spiritual events.
- **Visitor Services**:
  - Donation box for those wishing to contribute to the maintenance of the church.
  - Guided tours of the church are available upon request.
- **Description**: The Church of Agios Nikolaos is a central landmark in Skiathos Town. Known for its striking Byzantine icons and peaceful atmosphere, the church is a serene place for reflection and admiring religious art. The church is a key part of the town's spiritual and historical landscape, offering visitors an insight into Greek Orthodox traditions.

Skiathos Town is filled with rich history, stunning views, and vibrant street life. From the charming Old Town with its winding alleys to the lively port and key cultural landmarks, the town offers a unique experience that captures the essence of the island.

4.2 Beaches (Popular, Hidden Gems, Family-Friendly)

Skiathos is renowned for its pristine beaches, ranging from lively, bustling spots to quiet, secluded coves. The island boasts over 60 beaches, each with its own unique charm. Whether you're looking for popular sandy stretches, hidden gems, or family-friendly shores, Skiathos has something to offer every kind of beachgoer. Here's a detailed guide to some of the top beaches you can explore.

1. Koukounaries Beach (Popular Beach)

- **Location**: Located on the southwest coast of Skiathos, about 12 km from Skiathos Town.
- **Price**: Free to access; sunbeds and umbrellas available for rent at approximately €10-€15 per day.
- **Opening Hours**: Accessible year-round; beach bars open from 9:00 AM – 7:00 PM during the summer months.
- **Website**: No official website for the beach itself, but information available through Skiathos Tourism.
- **Key Features**:
    - Long, golden sandy beach with clear turquoise waters.
    - A mix of lively beach bars, tavernas, and water sports facilities.

- Surrounded by pine forests, providing a natural, serene backdrop.
- **Visitor Services**:
  - Sunbeds and umbrellas for rent.
  - Water sports including jet skiing, parasailing, and paddleboarding.
  - Numerous tavernas offering traditional Greek cuisine and fresh seafood.
  - Public restrooms and shower facilities.
- **Description**: Koukounaries Beach is one of the most famous beaches in Skiathos, known for its stunning beauty and vibrant atmosphere. The beach has shallow, calm waters, making it ideal for swimming. It's popular with both tourists and locals and offers a variety of amenities, including water sports and beachfront dining. The beach is surrounded by lush pine forests, which adds to its tranquil charm.

2. Lalaria Beach (Hidden Gem)

- **Location**: Situated on the northern coast of Skiathos, accessible only by boat.
- **Price**: Free to visit, boat trips cost approximately €20 €30 per person.
- **Opening Hours**: Accessible via boat tours; boat trips generally operate from 10:00 AM – 5:00 PM during the summer.
- **Website**: No official website; boat tour details can be found on local tour provider sites.
- **Key Features**:
  - Isolated and unspoiled, with dramatic white marble pebbles.
  - Crystal-clear waters perfect for snorkeling.
  - A backdrop of towering cliffs, creating a majestic atmosphere.
- **Visitor Services**:

- Boat tours to the beach are available from Skiathos Town and Koukounaries.
- No amenities at the beach itself; visitors should bring water and snacks.
- **Description**: Lalaria Beach is one of Skiathos' most iconic and secluded beaches, famous for its stunning white marble pebbles and dramatic backdrop of steep cliffs. The beach is only accessible by boat, which adds to its allure and makes it one of the most peaceful and hidden spots on the island. The crystal-clear waters are perfect for a refreshing swim or snorkeling among the rocky formations.

3. Banana Beach (Family-Friendly)

- **Location**: Located on the south coast of Skiathos, approximately 9 km from Skiathos Town.
- **Price**: Free to access; sunbeds and umbrellas available for rent at €10-€12 per day.
- **Opening Hours**: Open daily from 9:00 AM – 7:00 PM during the summer months.
- **Website**: No official website, but local tourism websites provide detailed information.
- **Key Features**:
  - Family-friendly beach with shallow, calm waters ideal for children.
  - A mix of sandy shore and areas with beach bars and tavernas.
  - A variety of water sports activities for both adults and children.
- **Visitor Services**:
  - Sunbeds and umbrellas for rent.
  - Water sports facilities, including banana boat rides and paddleboarding.
  - Restaurants and beach bars serving snacks, drinks, and traditional Greek dishes.
  - Restrooms and changing facilities available.
- **Description**: Banana Beach is one of the best family-friendly beaches on the island. It features shallow, clear waters that are safe for children to play in. The beach offers a more relaxed vibe than other popular spots, with several restaurants serving family-friendly meals. Water sports are available for those seeking adventure, but the overall atmosphere remains laid-back and welcoming.

4. Agia Eleni Beach (Hidden Gem)

- **Location**: Situated on the west coast of Skiathos, about 12 km from Skiathos Town.
- **Price**: Free to access; sunbeds and umbrellas are available for rent at approximately €8-€10 per day.

- **Opening Hours**: Open year-round; beach bars generally open from 9:00 AM – 7:00 PM in the summer.
- **Website**: No official website for the beach.
- **Key Features**:
  - A tranquil, more secluded beach with fine golden sand.
  - Clear, deep waters, perfect for swimming and snorkeling.
  - Ideal for a peaceful day away from the busier tourist beaches.
- **Visitor Services**:
  - Sunbeds and umbrellas available for rent.
  - A small beach bar offering drinks and snacks.
  - Limited amenities, so visitors should bring food and water for longer stays.
- **Description**: Agia Eleni Beach is a quieter, less crowded alternative to the more popular beaches on the island. Located on the west coast, it is ideal for those looking to relax in a peaceful setting. The beach is surrounded by pine trees and cliffs, offering a serene and secluded atmosphere. It's a great spot for those who enjoy swimming in calm waters or simply sunbathing in tranquility.

5. Vromolimnos Beach (Popular Beach)

- **Location**: Located on the south coast, about 10 km from Skiathos Town.
- **Price**: Free to access; sunbeds and umbrellas available for rent at €12-€15 per day.
- **Opening Hours**: Accessible year-round; beach bars operate from 9:00 AM – 7:00 PM during the summer.
- **Website**: No official website, but additional information is available through local tourism sites.
- **Key Features**:
  - A long sandy beach with shallow waters ideal for swimming.
  - Vibrant beach bars and restaurants offering a lively atmosphere.
  - Popular for water sports and boat rentals.
- **Visitor Services**:
  - Sunbeds and umbrellas for rent.
  - A wide range of water sports, including windsurfing, jet skiing, and parasailing.
  - Several restaurants and tavernas serving a variety of dishes.
  - Public restrooms and changing facilities.
- **Description**: Vromolimnos Beach is one of the most popular beaches on Skiathos, particularly loved by those who enjoy an active beach day. It's perfect for both relaxation and adventure, with opportunities for water sports like jet skiing and windsurfing. The shallow, warm waters are great for swimming, and

the surrounding area is lined with beach bars and restaurants, making it a lively yet laid-back spot for families and young travelers alike.

6. Achladies Beach (Family-Friendly)

- **Location**: Located just 3 km from Skiathos Town, on the eastern coast of the island.
- **Price**: Free to access; sunbeds and umbrellas available for rent at €7-€10 per day.
- **Opening Hours**: Open year-round; beach bars open from 9:00 AM – 7:00 PM in the summer.
- **Website**: No official website.
- **Key Features**:
  - Shallow waters ideal for children and non-swimmers.
  - Fine sand and clear, calm waters.
  - Family-friendly atmosphere with nearby amenities.
- **Visitor Services**:
  - Sunbeds and umbrellas available for rent.
  - A small selection of family-friendly tavernas and cafes nearby.
  - Restrooms and shower facilities available on-site.
- **Description**: Achladies Beach is perfect for families, featuring shallow waters and a gentle incline into the sea. It's a quieter, more relaxed beach compared to others on the island and offers a range of facilities including sunbeds, umbrellas, and nearby restaurants serving delicious local food. The calm, clear waters are ideal for children to play safely, and the beach is a great spot to enjoy a family day out by the sea.

Skiathos offers a diverse range of beaches, from lively hubs with water sports and restaurants to quiet retreats perfect for relaxation. Whether you're visiting with family, seeking adventure, or just wanting to soak in the natural beauty of the island, there's a beach in Skiathos to suit your needs.

4.3 Historical Sites and Landmarks (Monasteries, Churches, Forts)

Skiathos is not just a paradise for beach lovers; it also holds a wealth of historical sites and landmarks that showcase the island's rich cultural heritage. From ancient monasteries to Byzantine churches and Venetian forts, the island is a treasure trove of history waiting to be explored. Here's a detailed guide to some of the top historical sites and landmarks on Skiathos.

1. Monastery of Evangelistria

- **Location**: Located on the north side of Skiathos Island, approximately 4 km from Skiathos Town.
- **Price**: Free entry; donations are encouraged.
- **Opening Hours**: Daily, from 8:00 AM to 3:00 PM.
- **Website**: No official website.
- **Key Features**:
  - Historic monastery dating back to the 18th century.
  - Beautiful example of traditional Greek architecture.
  - Houses religious artifacts and important manuscripts.
  - Scenic views of the island and the surrounding area.
- **Visitor Services**:
  - Small gift shop offering religious items and souvenirs.
  - Restrooms and a small café.
  - Guided tours available in English and Greek (upon request).
- **Description**: The Monastery of Evangelistria is one of the most important religious sites on Skiathos. It was built in the early 18th century and has played a significant role in the island's religious and cultural history. The monastery is known for its well-preserved architecture, beautiful surroundings, and its connection to the Greek War of Independence (1821), where the local resistance was supported from this location. The monastery also hosts a museum that showcases religious icons, manuscripts, and artifacts. Visitors can enjoy a peaceful atmosphere, learn about the history of the island, and admire the stunning views.

2. Skiathos Castle (Kastro)

- **Location**: Located on the northern tip of Skiathos, 13 km from Skiathos Town.
- **Price**: €3 per person.
- **Opening Hours**: Daily, from 8:00 AM to 6:00 PM.
- **Website**: No official website.
- **Key Features**:
  - Venetian-era castle with panoramic views of the island and sea.
  - Historic site with ruins of old houses, churches, and defensive walls.
  - Once a refuge during pirate invasions in the 16th century.
- **Visitor Services**:
  - Informational signs in English and Greek around the site.
  - No official visitor services, so visitors should bring water and snacks.
  - Small parking area nearby.
- **Description**: Skiathos Castle, also known as Kastro, is one of the most iconic historical sites on the island. This ancient castle was built during the 14th century by the Venetians as a defensive structure to protect the inhabitants of Skiathos from pirate attacks. The castle is located on a hilltop, offering breathtaking panoramic views of the Aegean Sea. The ruins include parts of the castle walls, ancient houses, and the church of Agios Georgios. Although the area is largely uninhabited today, it remains an important site for history enthusiasts and those seeking stunning views. A hike up to the castle provides a sense of adventure along with historical intrigue.

3. Church of Agios Nikolaos (Skiathos Town)

- **Location**: In the heart of Skiathos Town, near the old port.
- **Price**: Free entry (donations are welcomed).
- **Opening Hours**: Open daily from 8:00 AM to 8:00 PM.
- **Website**: No official website.
- **Key Features**:
  - Beautiful example of traditional Greek Orthodox church architecture.
  - Revered for its stunning frescoes and religious significance.
  - Located in a vibrant area near the port, making it easily accessible.
- **Visitor Services**:
  - Informational pamphlets in Greek and English.
  - Nearby cafes and shops where visitors can relax after visiting the church.
  - A peaceful spot for reflection, with benches outside.
- **Description**: The Church of Agios Nikolaos is a prominent landmark in Skiathos Town, standing as a symbol of the island's spiritual life. The church is dedicated to St. Nicholas, the patron saint of sailors, which is fitting given

Skiathos' long history as a maritime hub. The church is admired for its intricate frescoes and its serene atmosphere. Visitors can enjoy both the interior's religious art and the peaceful surroundings, which offer an opportunity for quiet reflection. It's an essential stop for anyone exploring the spiritual heritage of Skiathos Town.

4. Monastery of Panagia Kounistra

- **Location**: Situated on the south coast of Skiathos, around 7 km from Skiathos Town.
- **Price**: Free entry; donations are welcome.
- **Opening Hours**: Open daily, from 9:00 AM to 1:00 PM and 4:00 PM to 6:00 PM.
- **Website**: No official website.
- **Key Features**:
  - A picturesque 19th-century monastery surrounded by olive groves.
  - Famous for its religious icons and panoramic views.
  - Offers a peaceful and quiet atmosphere for reflection.
- **Visitor Services**:
  - Small on-site gift shop selling religious icons and souvenirs.
  - Public restrooms are available.
  - A small café for refreshments after a visit.
- **Description**: The Monastery of Panagia Kounistra is located in a quiet and secluded part of Skiathos, making it a perfect place for those seeking peace and tranquility. Built in the 19th century, the monastery is dedicated to the Virgin Mary, and it is particularly known for its miraculous icon of the Virgin. The monastery is set among lush olive groves, providing a scenic backdrop. The church itself features a blend of traditional architecture and religious art. Visitors can also enjoy the spectacular views over the island and the Aegean Sea. This monastery is a serene escape from the bustling town and is perfect for spiritual scckcrs.

5. The Bourtzi Fortress (Skiathos Town)

- **Location**: Located on a small peninsula in Skiathos Town, accessible by a short walk or boat ride.
- **Price**: €3 per person.
- **Opening Hours**: Daily, from 9:00 AM to 6:00 PM.
- **Website**: No official website.
- **Key Features**:
  - Venetian-era fortress offering panoramic views of Skiathos Town and the surrounding sea.
  - A small museum with artifacts and displays about the island's history.

- A tranquil location with seating areas for relaxation.
- **Visitor Services**:
  - Small gift shop offering historical and cultural items.
  - A café/restaurant on-site, where visitors can enjoy refreshments while overlooking the water.
  - Public restrooms available.
- **Description**: The Bourtzi Fortress is a well-preserved Venetian fort located on a small peninsula just outside Skiathos Town. The fort was originally built to defend against pirates and later served as a military stronghold. Today, it is a quiet historical landmark where visitors can explore the remains of the fort, enjoy stunning views of the town and the harbor, and learn about the island's past. The small museum inside the fortress displays various historical artifacts, making it a fascinating spot for history lovers.

Skiathos' historical sites and landmarks offer a window into the island's rich cultural heritage. From Byzantine churches and Venetian forts to peaceful monasteries, these attractions provide a deeper understanding of the island's religious and historical significance. Whether you are exploring the Monastery of Evangelistria, wandering through the ruins of Skiathos Castle, or simply enjoying the serene atmosphere of the Monastery of Panagia Kounistra, Skiathos is a destination that appeals to both history enthusiasts and those seeking a cultural retreat.

4.4 Nature and Outdoors (Hiking, Walking Trails, Parks)

Skiathos is a paradise for nature enthusiasts, offering a wide range of outdoor activities set against stunning natural backdrops. From hiking trails that lead to breathtaking views to serene parks and protected nature areas, the island is perfect for those who want to explore its unspoiled landscapes. Below are the top nature and outdoor attractions in Skiathos that combine adventure with natural beauty.

1. Koukounaries Beach Nature Reserve

- **Location**: South-western part of Skiathos, near Koukounaries Beach.
- **Price**: Free entry.
- **Opening Hours**: Open daily, year-round.
- **Website**: No official website.
- **Key Features**:
  - A protected pine forest reserve next to Koukounaries Beach.
  - Home to a diverse array of flora and fauna.
  - Wetland area with a unique ecosystem, attracting many bird species.
- **Visitor Services**:

- Informational boards about the local wildlife and conservation efforts.
- Walking paths through the forest and along the wetland areas.
- Nearby cafes and tavernas for refreshments.

- **Description**: Koukounaries Beach Nature Reserve is one of the most important ecological sites on the island. The reserve is a lush pine forest that provides a peaceful escape from the busy beach and a sanctuary for wildlife. Visitors can enjoy leisurely walks through the forest while observing diverse plant species, birds, and other wildlife. The area is also home to a lagoon, making it an excellent location for birdwatching. The reserve's proximity to Koukounaries Beach means visitors can easily combine a nature walk with a relaxing day by the sea.

2. Skiathos Walking Trails

- **Location**: Various locations around the island, including Skiathos Town, Koukounaries, and the northern parts of the island.
- **Price**: Free entry.
- **Opening Hours**: Accessible year-round.
- **Website**: No official website, but detailed trail maps can be found in local tourist information offices.
- **Key Features**:
  - Over 30 km of marked hiking trails, offering a range of difficulty levels.
  - Scenic views of the Aegean Sea, lush forests, and traditional villages.
  - Trails for all skill levels, from easy coastal walks to challenging mountain hikes.
- **Visitor Services**:
  - Trail maps available at local tourist information offices and online platforms.
  - Guided tours available for more in-depth experiences.
  - Some trails pass through quaint villages where hikers can stop for a break and enjoy local food.
- **Description**: Skiathos is a wonderful island for hiking, with trails that cater to every level of walker, from casual strollers to avid trekkers. The island's walking trails offer fantastic opportunities to explore its natural beauty, including dense pine forests, olive groves, and rocky cliffs. One of the most popular trails is the route leading to the Monastery of Evangelistria, which offers stunning views of the island. Other trails wind through traditional villages, secluded beaches, and scenic hillsides, giving hikers a true sense of Skiathos' charm. Whether you want to take a short walk or embark on a full-day hike, Skiathos' walking trails are an excellent way to explore the island's diverse landscapes.

3. Mount Papas (Skiathos' Highest Peak)

- **Location**: The northern part of Skiathos, near the town of Skiathos.
- **Price**: Free entry.
- **Opening Hours**: Accessible year-round.
- **Website**: No official website.
- **Key Features**:
  - The highest point on Skiathos, standing at 432 meters (1,417 feet).
  - Panoramic views of the entire island and surrounding islands.
  - A rewarding hike with a moderate level of difficulty.
- **Visitor Services**:
  - Limited services on-site, but there are cafes and restaurants in the surrounding areas.
  - Trail markers help guide hikers to the summit.
- **Description**: Mount Papas is the highest peak on Skiathos, offering stunning views that extend across the entire island and beyond to the neighboring islands. A hike to the summit is moderately challenging but is a highly rewarding experience for those looking for a bit of adventure. The trail winds through dense forests of pine and olive trees, leading to the top where you're treated to spectacular vistas of Skiathos' beaches, towns, and neighboring islets. The summit is also home to a small chapel, adding to the peaceful, spiritual atmosphere of the area. Hikers should be prepared with water and sturdy shoes, but the hike is suitable for those with a good level of fitness.

4. Papadiamantis Park

- **Location**: In Skiathos Town, just a short walk from the Old Port.
- **Price**: Free entry.
- **Opening Hours**: Open daily from 8:00 AM to 8:00 PM.
- **Website**: No official website.
- **Key Features**:
  - A small urban park dedicated to the famous Greek writer Alexandros Papadiamantis.
  - Lush green space with benches and shaded areas for relaxation.
  - Perfect for a peaceful break in the middle of Skiathos Town.
- **Visitor Services**:
  - Informational plaques detailing the life and works of Papadiamantis.
  - Benches for resting and enjoying the quiet atmosphere.
  - Nearby cafes and shops.
- **Description**: Papadiamantis Park is a charming and tranquil green space located in the heart of Skiathos Town. The park is dedicated to the renowned Greek writer Alexandros Papadiamantis, who was born in Skiathos and became famous for his works reflecting Greek life and culture. The park is a peaceful

retreat where visitors can relax in the shade, read, or enjoy a quiet moment amidst the hustle and bustle of the town. It is an ideal place to take a break after a day of sightseeing, with plenty of benches and shaded spots to unwind.

5. The Skiathos Green Bus Routes and Nature

- **Location**: Various locations around Skiathos.
- **Price**: Bus tickets are around €2-3 per person.
- **Opening Hours**: Regular service throughout the day from 8:00 AM to 9:00 PM.
- **Website**: No official website, but routes and schedules are available at local tourist offices.
- **Key Features**:
  - A network of buses connecting key nature sites across Skiathos.
  - Easy access to beaches, parks, and trails.
  - Offers a relaxed and affordable way to explore Skiathos' natural beauty.
- **Visitor Services**:
  - Information about bus routes and schedules is available at hotels, the tourist office, and the bus stations.
  - Some buses have air conditioning and comfortable seating.
- **Description**: For those looking to explore Skiathos' nature without hiking, the island's Green Bus routes offer a great alternative. The buses connect many of the island's beautiful beaches, nature reserves, and forests, making it easy to explore the natural beauty of Skiathos without worrying about transportation. The Green Bus service is convenient, budget-friendly, and an excellent way to explore the island's scenic landscapes. Whether you're heading to Koukounaries Beach, the Monastery of Evangelistria, or one of the many other natural sites, the Green Bus offers an easy way to access some of the best outdoor experiences on the island.

Skiathos offers a wealth of outdoor activities for nature lovers, from hiking trails with spectacular views to serene parks and nature reserves. Whether you prefer a peaceful stroll through Papadiamantis Park, an adventurous hike to the summit of Mount Papas, or a day of birdwatching at Koukounaries Beach Nature Reserve, the island's natural attractions are a perfect complement to its vibrant cultural and historical offerings. These outdoor experiences allow visitors to connect with the island's stunning landscapes and enjoy its natural beauty to the fullest.

4.5 Museums and Art Galleries

Skiathos is rich in history, culture, and artistic expression. The island is home to several museums and art galleries that showcase its heritage, artistic legacy, and the beauty of its landscapes. From exhibitions dedicated to the island's famous writers to modern art collections, these cultural institutions offer visitors the opportunity to learn more about Skiathos' past and present through captivating exhibits. Below are some of the most notable museums and art galleries in Skiathos.

1. Skiathos Museum (Archaeological Museum of Skiathos)

- **Location**: Skiathos Town, on the main street near the Old Port.
- **Price**: €3 per adult, free for children under 18.
- **Opening Hours**:
  - Monday to Saturday: 9:00 AM to 3:00 PM.
  - Closed on Sundays and holidays.
- **Website**: [no official website]

- **Key Features**:
  - Artifacts from ancient times, including pottery, sculptures, and inscriptions.
  - Exhibits showcasing the island's role in Greek history.
  - Displays of ancient marble statues and mosaics.
- **Visitor Services**:
  - Informational boards in Greek and English.
  - Museum guide available for a small additional fee.
  - Small gift shop with books and souvenirs related to Skiathos' history.
- **Description**:
  The Archaeological Museum of Skiathos is the island's primary cultural institution, housing a rich collection of ancient artifacts from the island and surrounding areas. The museum's exhibits focus on the ancient Greek and Roman periods, showcasing pottery, sculptures, and inscriptions that offer a glimpse into the island's storied past. One of the highlights of the museum is the collection of sculptures from the Classical period, including a well-preserved marble bust of Alexander the Great. The museum is a must-visit for those interested in learning about the island's archaeological significance and ancient history.

2. Papadiamantis House Museum

- **Location**: Skiathos Town, on Papadiamantis Street, near the port.
- **Price**: €3 per adult, free for children under 18.
- **Opening Hours**:
  - Monday to Saturday: 9:00 AM to 3:00 PM.

- o Closed on Sundays.
- **Website**: [no official website]
- **Key Features**:
  - o The former home of Alexandros Papadiamantis, one of Greece's most famous authors.
  - o Exhibits on the life and works of Papadiamantis.
  - o A beautifully preserved house from the 19th century.
- **Visitor Services**:
  - o Guided tours available in Greek and English.
  - o Informational plaques in both Greek and English.
  - o Small gift shop with books, postcards, and other souvenirs related to Papadiamantis.
- **Description**:

  The Papadiamantis House Museum is dedicated to Alexandros Papadiamantis, who was born in Skiathos and became a renowned writer known for his vivid depictions of Greek life. The house has been preserved as it was when Papadiamantis lived there, and it offers an intimate look into his life and work. Visitors can explore the writer's personal belongings, including his writing desk and books, and learn more about his contributions to Greek literature. The museum is a literary gem and an essential stop for fans of Greek literature.

3. Skiathos Art Gallery

- **Location**: Skiathos Town, near the Old Port, on Papadiamantis Street.
- **Price**: Free entry.
- **Opening Hours**:
  - o Monday to Saturday: 10:00 AM to 2:00 PM and 6:00 PM to 9:00 PM.
  - o Closed on Sundays.
- **Website**: [no official website]
- **Key Features**:
  - o Contemporary art exhibitions by Greek and international artists.
  - o A variety of artistic mediums, including painting, sculpture, and photography.
  - o A focus on the cultural and artistic heritage of Skiathos and the surrounding Aegean region.
- **Visitor Services**:
  - o Information about ongoing exhibitions available at the entrance.
  - o Art sales and exhibitions open to the public.
  - o The opportunity to meet the artists during exhibition openings.
- **Description**:

  The Skiathos Art Gallery is a vibrant space dedicated to contemporary art, showcasing a wide range of works by both local and international artists. The gallery's exhibits focus on various artistic forms, from painting and photography to sculpture and mixed media. The gallery is known for its rotating exhibitions, making each visit a new experience. It is a great place for art lovers to immerse themselves in the local and international art scenes while also supporting emerging artists. The gallery is centrally located, making it easy to stop by while exploring Skiathos Town.

4. Skiathos Museum of Modern Art

- **Location**: Skiathos Town, at the entrance of the Old Port, opposite the Old Market.
- **Price**: €5 per adult, discounted prices for students and children.
- **Opening Hours**:
  - Daily: 10:00 AM to 4:00 PM.
- **Website**: [no official website]
- **Key Features**:
  - An extensive collection of modern and contemporary Greek art.
  - Works from the 20th and 21st centuries, including paintings, installations, and multimedia art.
  - Rotating exhibits with a focus on local and national artists.
- **Visitor Services**:
  - Audio guides available for a small fee, in Greek and English.
  - Art sales and catalogs available for purchase.
  - Workshops and artist talks periodically held at the museum.
- **Description**:
  The Skiathos Museum of Modern Art is a contemporary art institution that aims to bring modern Greek art to a broader audience. The museum features an impressive collection of works by renowned Greek artists, focusing on paintings, photography, and multimedia art. It offers an intimate look into the development of Greek art in the 20th and 21st centuries. The museum also hosts temporary exhibitions, providing visitors with the chance to experience fresh and innovative art from up-and-coming artists. Whether you are an art enthusiast or simply curious, this museum offers a fascinating insight into the world of modern Greek art.

5. The Folklore Museum of Skiathos

- **Location**: Skiathos Town, in the heart of the old town.
- **Price**: €2 per adult, free for children under 12.
- **Opening Hours**:
  - Monday to Saturday: 10:00 AM to 2:00 PM.

-     ○ Closed on Sundays.
- **Website**: [no official website]
- **Key Features**:
  - ○ A collection of traditional Greek artifacts, costumes, and tools.
  - ○ Displays about Skiathos' local history and way of life.
  - ○ A glimpse into the everyday life of past generations.
- **Visitor Services**:
  - ○ Informational plaques and descriptions in Greek and English.
  - ○ Periodic workshops on traditional Greek crafts.
  - ○ A small shop offering locally made goods and souvenirs.
- **Description**:

  The Folklore Museum of Skiathos provides a fascinating look at the island's rich cultural history. The museum houses a collection of traditional costumes, textiles, pottery, and household items from the past. Visitors can explore exhibits on local crafts, tools, and the island's agricultural heritage, gaining an understanding of the everyday life of the people who lived here. The museum is an excellent place to connect with Skiathos' past and appreciate the craftsmanship that has been passed down through generations.

Skiathos offers a vibrant cultural scene that is beautifully showcased in its museums and galleries. Whether you're interested in the island's ancient past, its literary history, or its modern artistic expressions, the museums of Skiathos provide an enriching experience for all types of visitors. From the quiet elegance of the Papadiamantis House Museum to the dynamic exhibitions at the Skiathos Art Gallery, there is something to captivate every visitor interested in the artistic and historical fabric of the island.

Chapter 5. Things to Do

5.1 Watersports and Adventure Activities (Kayaking, Windsurfing, Sailing)

Skiathos is renowned for its stunning coastlines, crystal-clear waters, and perfect weather, making it a prime destination for water-based activities. Whether you're seeking adventure or simply wish to relax by the sea, there are plenty of options for all levels of experience. From kayaking and windsurfing to sailing, the island offers endless opportunities to explore its beautiful coastline and vibrant marine life. Here's a closer look at some of the top watersports and adventure activities you can enjoy while visiting Skiathos.

1. Kayaking

- **Location**: Various beaches on the island, including Koukounaries, Banana Beach, and Megali Ammos.
- **Price**:
  - Single Kayak Rental: €15 per hour.
  - Tandem Kayak Rental: €25 per hour.
  - Guided Tours: €40 to €50 per person.
- **Opening Hours**: 9:00 AM to 6:00 PM (dependent on the provider).
- **Key Features**:
  - Calm waters ideal for beginners and families.
  - Opportunities to explore hidden coves and beaches.
  - Scenic coastal views and wildlife spotting, including dolphins and seabirds.
- **Visitor Services**:
  - Equipment rental (life jackets, paddles, and kayaks).
  - Professional guides offering guided tours around the island.
  - Safety briefings before departure.
  - Some locations offer photography services for your kayaking adventures.
- **Description**:
  Kayaking in Skiathos is a fantastic way to explore the island's coastline from a unique perspective. Paddle through tranquil waters, discover secluded beaches, and enjoy the stunning scenery of the island's rugged shoreline. The beaches of Koukounaries and Banana Beach are particularly popular for kayaking due to their calm, shallow waters. If you're looking for a bit more adventure, consider booking a guided kayaking tour, where you'll venture into less accessible areas of the island and enjoy the beauty of Skiathos away from the crowds. Whether

you're a beginner or an experienced kayaker, Skiathos offers options for everyone.

2. Windsurfing

- **Location**: Most popular spots include Koukounaries Beach, Megali Ammos, and Agia Paraskevi Beach.
- **Price**:
    - Equipment Rental: €30 to €50 per hour.
    - Windsurfing Lesson: €60 to €80 for 1 to 1.5 hours.
- **Opening Hours**: Typically from 9:00 AM to 7:00 PM (weather dependent).
- **Key Features**:
    - Ideal wind conditions for both beginners and experienced windsurfers.
    - Clear, warm waters perfect for practicing and exploring.
    - Specialized schools offering lessons and rentals.
- **Visitor Services**:
    - Windsurfing equipment rental (boards, sails, harnesses).
    - Group or private lessons for beginners and intermediates.
    - Safety gear including life vests and helmets.
    - Storage for personal equipment if you're a frequent windsurfer.
- **Description**:
  Windsurfing is one of the most exhilarating water sports in Skiathos, thanks to the island's consistent winds and crystal-clear waters. The island's beaches, especially Koukounaries, provide ideal conditions for both beginners and experienced windsurfers, with calm waters in the mornings and more challenging waves in the afternoons. Whether you're a first-timer looking to take a lesson or a seasoned windsurfer, Skiathos has plenty of providers that offer rentals and

lessons. Windsurfing is a great way to enjoy the Aegean Sea and experience the thrill of the wind and water.

3. Sailing

- **Location**: Sailing trips can depart from Skiathos Town, Koukounaries, or the Old Port.
- **Price**:
  - Private Charter: €150 to €400 per day (depending on the size and type of boat).
  - Group Sailing Tours: €40 to €70 per person (half-day tour).
  - Luxury Sailing (with skipper): €500+ per day.
- **Opening Hours**: Sailing trips are typically offered from 9:00 AM to sunset (depending on the provider).
- **Key Features**:
  - Explore hidden beaches, caves, and nearby islands such as Skopelos and Alonissos.
  - Private or group tours available.
  - Luxurious sailing experiences with catered meals or onboard services.
- **Visitor Services**:
  - Boat rental options with or without a skipper.
  - Half-day and full-day private charters available.
  - Group sailing trips to nearby islands and secluded beaches.
  - Catering services, including picnics or meals onboard, on private charters.

- **Description**:

Sailing around Skiathos is one of the most rewarding ways to experience the island's breathtaking coastline and surrounding areas. Charter a private yacht or join a group tour to explore the nearby islands of Skopelos and Alonissos. These islands are part of the Northern Sporades and are known for their rugged beauty and crystal-clear waters, ideal for swimming, snorkeling, and relaxing on secluded beaches. Whether you're looking to charter a private boat for a romantic day at sea or join a group tour to socialize and enjoy the landscape, there are plenty of options available for all kinds of budgets. The waters surrounding Skiathos are perfect for a peaceful and scenic day of sailing.

4. Stand-Up Paddleboarding (SUP)

- **Location**: Popular locations include Koukounaries, Vassilias, and Megali Ammos.
- **Price**:
  - SUP Rental: €15 to €30 per hour.
  - SUP Guided Tour: €40 to €60 per person (depending on duration and location).
- **Opening Hours**: 9:00 AM to 6:00 PM (weather dependent).
- **Key Features**:
  - Calm, clear waters ideal for beginners.
  - Rentals available for solo or tandem SUP boards.
  - Tours available for scenic exploration of the coast.
- **Visitor Services**:

- Paddleboard rentals and equipment, including life jackets and paddles.
- Guided tours for sightseeing and wildlife spotting.
- Lessons for beginners to get familiar with SUP techniques.

- **Description**:

 Stand-up paddleboarding (SUP) is a fun and low-impact way to explore Skiathos' waters. Whether you're a seasoned paddleboarder or a beginner, you'll find plenty of opportunities to enjoy the calm seas around Skiathos. Rent a board for an hour or take a guided tour to explore hidden beaches and caves that are inaccessible by land. SUP is also a great way to stay fit while enjoying the island's natural beauty, and many beaches offer rentals as well as lessons for those new to the sport.

5. Snorkeling and Scuba Diving

- **Location**: Popular diving spots include the waters around the island of Tsougria, the beaches near Skiathos Town, and the Kastro area.
- **Price**:
  - Snorkeling Trip: €30 to €50 per person.
  - Scuba Diving Lesson: €80 to €120 per person (beginner course).
  - Scuba Diving Trip (guided): €60 to €100 per person.
- **Opening Hours**: Dependent on the provider, usually from 9:00 AM to 6:00 PM.
- **Key Features**:
  - Rich marine life, including colorful fish and sea turtles.

- ○ Clear waters ideal for visibility.
- ○ Professional guides and instructors available for diving experiences.
- **Visitor Services**:
  - ○ Guided snorkeling and scuba trips.
  - ○ Rental of diving equipment (masks, fins, wetsuits).
  - ○ Certified instructors for first-time divers.
- **Description**:

  Skiathos is home to some of the most beautiful waters in Greece, offering excellent conditions for both snorkeling and scuba diving. The island's marine life is diverse, with opportunities to spot sea turtles, schools of fish, and even ancient shipwrecks while diving. Whether you're a first-time diver or an experienced one, there are plenty of certified diving centers offering guided trips and courses. For those who prefer to stay closer to the surface, snorkeling is a great alternative, and Skiathos offers some of the clearest waters for an unforgettable underwater experience.

Skiathos offers a rich variety of water-based activities for all levels of adventurers. Whether you're kayaking through its peaceful coves, windsurfing on the Aegean Sea, or sailing to nearby islands, the possibilities are endless. Watersports are one of the best ways to discover the island's stunning natural beauty while enjoying the warm Greek sun and clear waters. With professional instructors, high-quality equipment rentals, and pristine surroundings, Skiathos provides an unforgettable experience for water sport enthusiasts.

5.2 Boat Tours and Island Cruises

Skiathos, with its rich coastline, crystal-clear waters, and surrounding islands, is a prime destination for boat tours and island cruises. Exploring the Aegean Sea by boat allows you to visit remote beaches, hidden coves, and neighboring islands that are otherwise inaccessible by land. Whether you are seeking a leisurely cruise, a private yacht experience, or an adventurous day trip, Skiathos offers a wide range of boat tours and island cruises suited to every traveler's needs.

1. Half-Day and Full-Day Island Cruises

- **Location**: Departures typically from Skiathos Town or the Old Port.
- **Price**:
  - ○ Half-Day Cruise: €30 to €50 per person.
  - ○ Full-Day Cruise: €50 to €100 per person.
- **Opening Hours**: Departures usually between 9:00 AM and 10:00 AM, returning in the afternoon (half-day) or late afternoon (full-day).

- **Key Features**:
  - Explore Skiathos' hidden gems, nearby islands (Skopelos, Alonissos), and secluded beaches.
  - Opportunities for swimming, snorkeling, and relaxing.
  - Guided tours with English-speaking captains and crew.
  - Group tours or private charters available.
- **Visitor Services**:
  - Complimentary refreshments, including water, soft drinks, and sometimes snacks or lunch (depending on the tour).
  - Onboard amenities, such as sunbeds and shaded areas.
  - Safety equipment (life jackets, first aid kits).
  - Snorkeling gear (some tours provide equipment for water activities).
- **Description**:
  The half-day and full-day island cruises around Skiathos provide a relaxed yet adventurous way to explore the island's coast and nearby destinations. A popular cruise option includes visiting Skopelos and Alonissos, two islands renowned for their pristine natural beauty. Many of these cruises offer time for swimming, snorkeling, and sunbathing in secluded areas away from the crowds. If you're seeking a more intimate experience, private charters are available where you can enjoy a more personalized journey with options for meals onboard, music, and customized itineraries. A cruise along Skiathos' coast offers stunning views of the island's lush landscape, cliffs, and crystal-clear waters.

2. Private Yacht Charters

- **Location**: Skiathos Town, Skiathos Old Port, Koukounaries Beach.
- **Price**:
  - Private Yacht Charter: €300 to €1,000+ per day (depending on the yacht's size and amenities).
  - Skippered Yacht Charters (with crew): €600 to €1,500 per day.
- **Opening Hours**: Flexible, available throughout the day with customizable start times.
- **Key Features**:
  - Exclusive, private experience for you and your group.
  - Luxury yachts with spacious decks, sunbeds, and shaded areas.
  - Option for onboard meals (with catering) or picnics.
  - Personalized itineraries to explore the Aegean Sea, including private beaches, caves, and nearby islands.
- **Visitor Services**:

- o Skipper and crew (optional).
- o Water toys and equipment, including snorkeling gear, paddleboards, and jet skis.
- o Meals, drinks, and catering options onboard.
- o Personalized service based on your preferences.
- **Description**:

  For those looking to experience Skiathos in ultimate luxury, a private yacht charter is the way to go. Whether you're celebrating a special occasion, enjoying a romantic getaway, or just seeking the freedom of the open sea, private yacht charters offer unparalleled experiences. You can choose your departure time, itinerary, and even the type of yacht you want to sail on, with options ranging from sleek motorboats to lavish sailboats. Your skipper will guide you to hidden gems along Skiathos' coastline and to nearby islands like Skopelos, Alonissos, and the uninhabited island of Tsougria, where you can stop for a swim, lunch, or simply relax on the water. Many charters also offer luxurious onboard amenities such as meals prepared by private chefs, refreshing drinks, and water sports equipment.

3. Sunset Cruises

- **Location**: Depart from Skiathos Town or the Old Port.
- **Price**:
  - o Sunset Cruise: €40 to €70 per person.
- **Opening Hours**: 5:00 PM to sunset (timing varies depending on the season).
- **Key Features**:
  - o Experience breathtaking sunsets over the Aegean Sea.
  - o Tranquil atmosphere with less crowded conditions.
  - o Small group sizes for a more intimate experience.
  - o Scenic views of the coastline, with stops for a swim or a drink.
- **Visitor Services**:
  - o Light snacks or dinner onboard (some cruises offer full meals).
  - o Drinks, including cocktails, or soft drinks.
  - o Onboard music and relaxing ambiance.
- **Description**:

  Sunset cruises are one of the most romantic and peaceful ways to experience Skiathos and its neighboring islands. As you sail out into the crystal-clear waters, you'll be treated to a front-row seat to the stunning sunset over the Aegean Sea. The glowing sky and the surrounding islands create an unforgettable backdrop for your journey. Most sunset cruises include a relaxing sail around Skiathos' coastline, with an opportunity for swimming or snorkeling in quiet coves before enjoying the breathtaking views as the sun sets. It's the perfect way to unwind and enjoy the tranquility of the sea while savoring a refreshing drink and light bites.

4. Skopelos & Alonissos Day Trips

- **Location**: Depart from Skiathos Town, Koukounaries, or other major ports.
- **Price**:
  - Day Trip: €40 to €80 per person.
  - Private Trip: €200 to €500 (depending on the boat).
- **Opening Hours**: Full-day trips, typically departing at 9:00 AM and returning by 6:00 PM.
- **Key Features**:
  - Explore the picturesque islands of Skopelos and Alonissos, including beaches, traditional villages, and nature reserves.
  - Guided tours with historical insights into each island's culture.
  - Time for swimming, hiking, and exploring the islands.
- **Visitor Services**:
  - Onboard services such as drinks, snacks, and sometimes lunch.
  - Guided tours of Skopelos' medieval village or Alonissos' National Marine Park.
  - Stopovers at secluded beaches for relaxation and swimming.
- **Description**:
  Skopelos and Alonissos are two of the most beautiful and peaceful islands in the Northern Sporades, and a day trip to these islands is a must-do when visiting Skiathos. These day trips usually combine a sail around the islands' coastlines, with stops at picturesque beaches and quaint villages. Skopelos, famously known as the filming location for the movie *Mamma Mia!*, is full of lush greenery and idyllic old towns. Alonissos, known for its protected marine park, is a haven for nature lovers, offering chances to spot seals and dolphins. These day trips provide a perfect blend of natural beauty, culture, and adventure.

Boat tours and island cruises are a fantastic way to explore the stunning landscapes around Skiathos and its neighboring islands. Whether you're seeking a peaceful sunset cruise, a full-day excursion to Skopelos and Alonissos, or a private yacht charter for an exclusive experience, Skiathos offers plenty of options to suit all tastes and budgets. From the freedom of exploring at your own pace to guided tours with knowledgeable skippers, the Aegean Sea promises an unforgettable adventure for all visitors.

5.3 Cultural Experiences (Music Festivals, Dance, Arts)

Skiathos is a culturally rich island that blends its natural beauty with a vibrant arts scene, traditional Greek music, and lively festivals. Visitors to the island can immerse themselves in the local culture through music festivals, traditional dances, art exhibitions, and much more. Whether you're a fan of classical music, folk traditions, or modern art, Skiathos has a range of cultural experiences that cater to all tastes.

1. Skiathos Summer Festival

- **Location**: Various venues around Skiathos Town, including the Skiathos Town Theatre and open-air venues.
- **Price**:
  - Tickets range from €10 to €50, depending on the event (discounts for students and seniors available).
- **Opening Hours**:
  - Typically held from late June to early September. Events are held in the evenings, starting at around 8:00 PM.
- **Key Features**:
  - A series of concerts, theatrical performances, and art exhibitions.
  - Features local and international artists performing in a variety of genres, including classical music, opera, jazz, and traditional Greek folk music.
  - Outdoor performances in picturesque settings.
- **Visitor Services**:
  - Tickets available online or at local tourist information centers.
  - Some venues offer refreshments and food during intermissions.
  - English-speaking staff at major event venues.
- **Description**:
  The Skiathos Summer Festival is one of the island's most celebrated cultural events, offering a vibrant program of music, theatre, and dance performances. Throughout the summer, the festival brings world-class performers to the island, with a particular focus on classical music and jazz. It is an excellent opportunity to experience the fusion of Greek and international culture, all set against the beautiful backdrop of Skiathos' charming venues, including its historical theatres and scenic outdoor spaces. Don't miss out on performances that feature famous composers, as well as local Greek musicians and dancers.

2. Traditional Greek Music and Dance

- **Location**: Various tavernas and venues around Skiathos Town and the island's villages.

- **Price**:
  - Free entry at some tavernas; prices for dinner and drinks range from €15 to €40 per person.
- **Opening Hours**:
  - Most performances take place in the evening, between 8:00 PM and 11:00 PM.
- **Key Features**:
  - Experience traditional Greek music, including bouzouki performances and folk dancing.
  - Local tavernas host regular live music nights showcasing Greek classics and contemporary hits.
  - Enjoy local food, and a friendly, welcoming atmosphere.
- **Visitor Services**:
  - Some venues offer dinner packages with performances.
  - Greek music lessons or dance workshops may be available at certain venues.
- **Description**:
  Skiathos' cultural heritage is deeply tied to Greek music and dance, and visitors can enjoy live performances in many of the island's tavernas and cultural centers. Traditional Greek music, often played on the bouzouki, fills the air during dinner hours, creating a festive atmosphere. Local musicians perform popular songs, including regional folk music, alongside more contemporary Greek tunes. For a more hands-on experience, some venues also offer opportunities to learn traditional Greek dances, such as the famous "Sirtaki," and join in the fun.

3. Skiathos Art Gallery and Local Artists

- **Location**: Skiathos Town, near the Old Port and in various gallery spaces around the island.
- **Price**:
  - Free entry to most galleries; special exhibitions may charge entry fees ranging from €5 to €10.
- **Opening Hours**:
  - Most galleries are open daily from 10:00 AM to 7:00 PM, with extended hours during the summer months.
- **Key Features**:
  - Exhibitions showcasing local and international artists.
  - A mix of contemporary art, traditional Greek art, and photography.

- ○ Art workshops and interactive exhibitions.
- **Visitor Services**:
  - ○ Art pieces available for purchase.
  - ○ Guided tours are available upon request.
  - ○ Art workshops and events for visitors interested in learning more about Greek artistic traditions.
- **Description**:

  Skiathos has a burgeoning art scene, and visitors can explore several galleries that showcase both local and international works. The Skiathos Art Gallery, located in the heart of Skiathos Town, regularly hosts rotating exhibitions that include paintings, sculptures, and photography. Local artists often display works inspired by the island's stunning landscapes, rich cultural heritage, and maritime history. For those interested in a deeper cultural experience, some galleries also offer workshops where you can learn traditional Greek crafts, including pottery, weaving, and painting.

4. Skiathos International Film Festival

- **Location**: Various venues in Skiathos Town, with screenings held in open-air cinemas and local theatres.
- **Price**:
  - ○ Tickets typically range from €5 to €15 per person.
- **Opening Hours**:
  - ○ Held annually, usually in late August or early September, with screenings starting at 9:00 PM.
- **Key Features**:
  - ○ Screening of international films, including Greek cinema, independent films, and documentaries.
  - ○ Special focus on film-making, with masterclasses and panel discussions with filmmakers.
  - ○ Open-air cinemas providing a unique movie-watching experience under the stars.
- **Visitor Services**:
  - ○ English-subtitled films are available for most screenings.
  - ○ Refreshments available at cinema venues.
- **Description**:

  The Skiathos International Film Festival is an important event for film enthusiasts. The festival showcases a diverse range of international films, from major releases to independent projects, with a special emphasis on Greek cinema. This event is an excellent opportunity to experience the cinematic arts in a relaxed and informal setting. Visitors can enjoy the films at one of the island's open-air cinemas, where the stars above create an unforgettable movie-watching atmosphere. The festival also organizes workshops and discussions with filmmakers, allowing visitors to learn more about the film industry.

5. Local Craft Markets

- **Location**: Skiathos Town and surrounding villages.
- **Price**:
  - Free entry to the markets; prices for crafts vary, with handmade items priced between €5 and €50.
- **Opening Hours**:
  - Markets are generally open from 9:00 AM to 6:00 PM, with extended hours during peak tourist season.
- **Key Features**:
  - Handmade crafts, jewelry, pottery, and local products.
  - Interaction with local artisans who create unique, one-of-a-kind pieces.
  - Souvenirs reflecting the island's culture and heritage.
- **Visitor Services**:
  - Some market vendors may offer workshops on traditional crafts, such as pottery making and embroidery.
  - Items available for purchase as souvenirs.
- **Description**:
  For a taste of Skiathos' local arts and crafts, visiting the island's markets is a must. The markets offer a wide range of handmade items, including pottery, jewelry, textiles, and local food products. Visitors can meet the artisans who create these works and gain insight into the traditional techniques passed down through generations. Many of the items sold at the markets are unique and make for perfect souvenirs that carry the spirit of the island with you. Some markets even offer hands-on experiences where you can learn the art of pottery or other traditional crafts.

Skiathos offers a wealth of cultural experiences that allow visitors to dive deep into the island's rich history, music, art, and traditions. Whether you're attending the Skiathos Summer Festival, enjoying a live music performance, or exploring local art galleries, there's always something to connect with on a cultural level. Skiathos' cultural offerings make it not just a destination for sun and sea but also a vibrant hub for those interested in the arts, local traditions, and Greek heritage.

5.4 Day Trips and Excursions (Nearby Islands, Skiathos' Hidden Treasures)

Skiathos, with its idyllic landscapes and serene beaches, offers not only incredible experiences on the island itself but also a perfect base for exploring nearby islands and hidden gems. Whether you're looking for a peaceful day of exploration or a thrilling adventure, there's a variety of day trips and excursions that will reveal the beauty of the region. Here's a guide to the most popular and unique day trips and excursions around Skiathos.

1. Day Trip to Skopelos Island

- **Location**: Skopelos, a nearby island in the Northern Sporades archipelago.
- **Price**:
  - Ferry tickets: Around €10 to €15 each way.
  - Excursion packages (including guided tours, meals): Around €40 to €70 per person.
- **Travel Time**:
  - Approximately 1 hour by ferry from Skiathos.
- **Key Features**:
  - Skopelos is known for its lush pine forests, crystal-clear waters, and picturesque villages.
  - Famous as the filming location for the movie *Mamma Mia!*, with many iconic spots from the film available to visit.
  - Traditional Greek architecture, olive groves, and tranquil beaches.
- **Visitor Services**:
  - Ferry services run daily between Skiathos and Skopelos, with seasonal timetables available online.
  - Guided tours are available, offering insight into the island's history and filming locations.
- **Description**:
  A day trip to Skopelos is a fantastic way to experience a quieter, less-touristy island while enjoying the same stunning beauty as Skiathos. Skopelos offers a combination of serene beaches, charming villages, and natural wonders. Visit the Agios Ioannis chapel, famous for its appearance in *Mamma Mia!*, or explore the island's medieval castle. For nature lovers, hiking trails lead through dense pine forests, offering breathtaking views. With several secluded beaches, including Panormos and Kastani, Skopelos is perfect for a peaceful escape from the crowds.

2. Day Trip to Alonissos Island

- **Location**: Alonissos, part of the Northern Sporades.
- **Price**:
  - Ferry tickets: Approximately €15 to €20 each way.
  - Excursion packages (including lunch and guided tours): Around €50 to €80 per person.
- **Travel Time**:
  - About 1.5 hours by ferry from Skiathos.
- **Key Features**:
  - Known for its stunning natural environment, Alonissos is home to the Alonissos Marine Park, Greece's first marine protected area.
  - Whitewashed houses, crystal-clear waters, and unspoiled beaches.
  - Great for hiking, birdwatching, and discovering unique wildlife.
- **Visitor Services**:
  - Daily ferry services to Alonissos with options for guided tours.
  - Visitors can rent kayaks or small boats for exploring secluded coves.
- **Description**:

  Alonissos is a haven for nature enthusiasts and those seeking an escape into unspoiled landscapes. The island is home to the Mediterranean monk seal, which can be spotted around the protected marine park. Alonissos is also famous for its beautiful beaches, including Agios Dimitrios and Leftos Gialos. For history buffs, the old village of Alonissos (Chora) offers charming stone streets and traditional architecture. This day trip is perfect for those who enjoy outdoor activities, such as hiking through the island's rugged hills or taking a boat trip to explore nearby caves and secluded beaches.

3. Day Trip to Skiathos' Hidden Beaches and Coves

- **Location**: Various hidden beaches and coves along Skiathos' coastline.
- **Price**:
  - Boat tours: Around €30 to €50 per person, depending on the length and inclusivity of the tour.
  - Private boat rentals: Starting at €100 for a half-day.
- **Key Features**:
  - Skiathos is home to many less-accessible, hidden beaches that are perfect for a peaceful day of relaxation.
  - Secluded coves like Lalaria Beach, accessible only by boat, offer stunning views and crystal-clear waters.
  - Perfect for swimming, sunbathing, or snorkeling in a quiet, private setting.
- **Visitor Services**:
  - Boat tours often include a captain and offer refreshments, beach towels, and snacks.

○ Private boat rentals can be arranged with or without a skipper.

- **Description**:

  For those seeking to explore Skiathos' less crowded and untouched beauty, a day trip to its hidden beaches is the perfect option. A boat ride to Lalaria Beach will take you to one of the most scenic spots on the island, where you can admire the famous white cliffs and enjoy a refreshing swim in turquoise waters. The beach is only accessible by boat, making it an exclusive experience. You can also explore other hidden coves such as Kastro Beach, reachable by boat or a scenic hike. These beaches offer a tranquil and picturesque setting, ideal for escaping the crowds.

4. Day Trip to Tsougria Island

- **Location**: Tsougria, a small uninhabited island located just off the coast of Skiathos.
- **Price**:
  ○ Boat ride: Approximately €10 to €15 for a round-trip per person.
  ○ Private boat rentals: Around €50 to €80 for a half-day trip.
- **Travel Time**:
  ○ Just 15 minutes by boat from Skiathos Town.
- **Key Features**:
  ○ A secluded, peaceful island with sandy beaches and crystal-clear waters.
  ○ Ideal for snorkeling, swimming, and relaxing in a serene environment.
  ○ No commercial development, offering a truly natural experience.
- **Visitor Services**:
  ○ Limited services on the island; visitors must bring their own food and drinks.
  ○ Boat tours often provide essentials such as snacks and refreshments.
- **Description**:

  Tsougria Island is a small gem, just a short boat ride from Skiathos, offering a secluded escape from the hustle and bustle of the main island. With no hotels or shops, Tsougria is an ideal destination for those seeking a quiet retreat. Visitors can relax on its pristine beaches or snorkel in the clear waters to discover the underwater life. The island is perfect for a day of peaceful relaxation and offers excellent opportunities for picnics and private beach days.

5. Skiathos Town and Kastro Ruins Excursion

- **Location**: Kastro, a medieval settlement located on the northwestern tip of Skiathos.
- **Price**:

- ○ Excursion packages (including transportation, guide, and lunch): Around €40 to €60 per person.
- ○ Hiking: Free access to the ruins; transportation by taxi or boat costs around €15 to €20 per person.
- **Opening Hours**:
  - ○ The ruins are open daily, with no set opening hours, but best visited in the morning or late afternoon.
- **Key Features**:
  - ○ The Kastro ruins, a former Venetian fortress dating back to the 14th century.
  - ○ Stunning views of the Aegean Sea and surrounding islands.
  - ○ Opportunity to explore a historical and archaeological site.
- **Visitor Services**:
  - ○ Guided tours of the Kastro ruins are available.
  - ○ Boat trips can be arranged from Skiathos Town or from other beaches.
- **Description**:
  A visit to the Kastro ruins is a journey back in time. The ancient settlement, once the capital of Skiathos, offers a glimpse into the island's rich history. The site is perched on a rocky hill, providing spectacular views over the Aegean Sea. You can hike to the ruins or take a boat excursion to explore the area in a more relaxed manner. The remnants of the old walls, churches, and houses are spread throughout the site, and the location is perfect for photography or simply enjoying the peaceful atmosphere.

Whether you're exploring the quiet beaches of Skopelos, the rugged nature of Alonissos, or uncovering Skiathos' hidden treasures, there's no shortage of incredible day trips to enjoy. These excursions not only offer a chance to discover nearby islands but also provide unforgettable experiences immersed in nature, culture, and history. Every trip from Skiathos unveils a new aspect of the Northern Sporades, ensuring that your time on the island will be filled with diverse and enriching experiences.

5.5 Shopping (Local Markets, Boutiques, Souvenirs)

Skiathos is a wonderful destination not just for its natural beauty but also for its unique shopping opportunities. Whether you're looking for a traditional Greek souvenir, a stylish boutique item, or local handmade crafts, the island offers a variety of shopping experiences to suit all tastes. Here's a guide to the best shopping spots, including local markets, boutiques, and souvenir stores, to help you take a piece of Skiathos home.

1. Skiathos Town: The Heart of Shopping

- **Location**: Skiathos Town, the island's bustling capital.
- **Price**:
  - Local souvenirs: €5 to €25.
  - Handmade jewelry and accessories: €10 to €50.
  - Fashion boutiques: €30 to €150 depending on the brand.
- **Opening Hours**:
  - Most shops are open from 9:00 AM to 1:30 PM and 5:00 PM to 9:00 PM, with extended hours during peak season.
- **Key Features**:
  - A mix of traditional Greek souvenir shops, high-end boutiques, and artisan stores.
  - The streets of Skiathos Town are lined with charming stores selling local products such as handmade ceramics, jewelry, olive oil, and textiles.
  - Great for fashion lovers, with boutique shops offering stylish clothing and accessories.
- **Visitor Services**:
  - Personalized shopping experiences available in certain high-end boutiques.
  - Friendly shopkeepers often speak English and can offer recommendations.
- **Description**:
  Skiathos Town is the ideal spot for an afternoon of shopping. The town's winding streets are home to a range of stores offering everything from stylish clothing to local handicrafts. The traditional Greek market area, with its quaint shops, is perfect for finding unique souvenirs like woven scarves, handcrafted jewelry, and traditional Greek sandals. For those seeking something more upscale, Skiathos Town has a selection of high-end boutiques featuring Greek and international fashion brands. Don't forget to explore the many stores selling local olive oil, honey, herbs, and spices – all perfect for taking home as gifts or personal keepsakes.

2. Papadiamantis Street: A Shopping Mecca

- **Location**: Papadiamantis Street, Skiathos Town.
- **Price**:
  - Souvenirs and trinkets: €5 to €30.
  - Local crafts: €10 to €50.
- **Opening Hours**:
  - Typically 10:00 AM to 9:00 PM, with extended hours in summer.

- **Key Features**:
  - Named after the famous Greek writer Alexandros Papadiamantis, this street is the shopping hub of Skiathos Town.
  - The street features a blend of traditional and contemporary shops, including local artisan boutiques, gift shops, and perfumeries.
  - It's also home to several Greek coffee shops, where you can take a break after a day of shopping.
- **Visitor Services**:
  - Many shops offer free gift wrapping.
  - Locally-owned businesses offer products that support the island's community.
- **Description**:
  Papadiamantis Street is a must-visit for shoppers on Skiathos. Known for its lively atmosphere, this pedestrianized street is lined with shops offering an array of local goods. Visitors will find unique souvenirs, from ceramic plates and hand-painted icons to colorful textiles and woven baskets. For fashion lovers, several boutiques sell contemporary Greek clothing brands, perfect for adding some local style to your wardrobe. Papadiamantis Street is also the place to find traditional Greek perfumes, which make for a fragrant and memorable gift.

3. Local Markets and Street Vendors

- **Location**: Skiathos Town, particularly around the Old Port and the waterfront areas.
- **Price**:
  - Handcrafted souvenirs: €5 to €20.
  - Fresh local produce (olive oil, honey, herbs): €3 to €15.
- **Opening Hours**:
  - Most markets operate from 8:00 AM to 2:00 PM, especially on weekends.
- **Key Features**:
  - Vibrant, open-air markets where you can find a variety of local produce, handmade goods, and fresh herbs.
  - Vendors often offer samples of their products, such as olives, cheeses, and honey.
  - Bargaining is common, making it an enjoyable experience for shoppers.
- **Visitor Services**:
  - Some markets offer organized tours or tastings, especially for local food products.
  - Many vendors accept credit cards, but it's advisable to carry cash for smaller purchases.

- **Description**:

  For those who enjoy a more traditional shopping experience, the local markets around Skiathos Town offer an authentic glimpse into island life. In the markets, you'll find a mix of fresh local produce, handmade crafts, and artisan products. Popular items to look out for include locally produced olive oil, wild herbs, and aromatic honey. The vibrant colors and smells of these markets make for an exciting shopping experience, while the friendly vendors will share their knowledge about the island's agricultural history. It's also a great place to pick up a quick souvenir at a lower price.

4. Boutiques and Artisan Shops in Troulos

- **Location**: Troulos, a village located in the southern part of Skiathos.
- **Price**:
  - Handmade leather goods: €15 to €40.
  - Artisan jewelry: €10 to €50.
- **Opening Hours**:
  - Shops are open from 10:00 AM to 7:00 PM, with extended hours during the summer months.
- **Key Features**:
  - Troulos offers a quieter shopping experience compared to Skiathos Town, with boutiques selling unique artisan crafts, including leather goods, jewelry, and clothing.
  - Some stores offer locally made products, from handwoven textiles to handcrafted wooden items.
- **Visitor Services**:
  - Personal shopping assistance from local artisans, who are happy to share the story behind their work.
- **Description**:

  Troulos is a peaceful village that offers a more laid-back shopping experience compared to the busier Skiathos Town. Many of the boutiques in this area feature locally made goods, from hand-stitched leather bags and belts to intricate jewelry pieces made by local artisans. Whether you're searching for something stylish or unique, the shops in Troulos offer a great selection of one-of-a-kind items that reflect the island's craft traditions.

5. Souvenir Shops at the Skiathos Port

- **Location**: Skiathos Port, located at the heart of the town.
- **Price**:
  - Keychains, postcards, and small souvenirs: €2 to €10.
  - Local handicrafts: €10 to €30.

- **Opening Hours**:
  - Open daily, usually from 9:00 AM to 9:00 PM.
- **Key Features**:
  - A wide selection of small souvenirs such as postcards, keychains, and magnets, perfect for gifts or memories.
  - Several shops at the port sell handmade crafts and local delicacies.
- **Visitor Services**:
  - Many shops offer quick and easy purchases for tourists arriving and departing the island.
- **Description**:

  The shops around Skiathos Port are ideal for tourists looking for a quick and easy souvenir. These shops offer a variety of items, from small mementos like keychains and magnets to local Greek products like olive oil, honey, and ceramics. It's an excellent spot for grabbing a gift for someone back home or a keepsake from your time in Skiathos.

Shopping in Skiathos offers a mix of traditional Greek crafts, modern fashion, and unique local products, perfect for bringing a piece of the island back home. From charming boutiques in Skiathos Town to artisan shops in Troulos, there's something for every shopper. Whether you're after a handcrafted piece of jewelry, a bottle of local olive oil, or simply a fun souvenir, the island's shopping scene will enhance your experience and give you a deeper connection to its culture.

Chapter 6. Dining and Nightlife

6.1 Traditional Greek Cuisine (Must-Try Dishes, Local Specialties)

Greek cuisine is an integral part of Skiathos' cultural identity, with traditional dishes that showcase the island's rich agricultural and maritime heritage. Dining in Skiathos offers a delightful experience, blending fresh, local ingredients with centuries-old recipes. Whether you're enjoying a meal by the beach or in the charming streets of Skiathos Town, the food will leave you wanting more. Here's a guide to the must-try dishes and local specialties in Skiathos.

1. Souvlaki and Gyros

- **Location**: Found at most tavernas, restaurants, and street food stalls across the island.
- **Price**:
  - Souvlaki: €4 to €8.
  - Gyros: €4 to €7.
- **Description**:
  These two iconic Greek fast foods are a must-try during your visit to Skiathos. Souvlaki consists of skewered and grilled meat (usually pork, chicken, or lamb) served with pita bread, salad, and a variety of sauces. Gyros is similar, but the meat is cooked on a vertical rotisserie, giving it a distinct flavor. Both are often served with tzatziki (yogurt and cucumber dip), fries, and fresh vegetables.
- **Key Features**:
  - Best enjoyed with a cold drink in a lively setting.
  - Perfect for a quick, satisfying meal on the go.

2. Moussaka

- **Location**: Available at most traditional Greek tavernas.
- **Price**: €8 to €12.
- **Description**:
  Moussaka is one of the most beloved Greek dishes and a staple of Skiathos cuisine. This rich, layered casserole consists of eggplant, minced meat (usually lamb or beef), béchamel sauce, and spices. It is baked to golden perfection and often served as a main course during lunch or dinner.
- **Key Features**:
  - Hearty and filling, making it a perfect choice for dinner.
  - Often served with a side of fresh salad or vegetables.

- **Tip**: Look for family-owned tavernas that offer homemade moussaka for an authentic experience.

3. Local Seafood (Fresh Fish, Calamari, Octopus)

- **Location**: Taverns and restaurants by the sea, particularly in Skiathos Town and along the coast.
- **Price**:
  - Grilled fish: €12 to €20.
  - Calamari: €10 to €15.
  - Octopus: €12 to €18.
- **Description**:
  Being an island, Skiathos offers some of the freshest seafood in Greece. Grilled fish (such as sea bream or red snapper) is a local favorite, often served with lemon and olive oil. Calamari (squid) and octopus are also popular, typically grilled or served in a rich tomato-based sauce. Dining by the sea provides the perfect ambiance for enjoying these dishes.
- **Key Features**:
  - Best enjoyed fresh and prepared with simple, high-quality ingredients.

4. Skiathos' Specialties: Bougatsa and Skiathos Cheese Pie

- **Location**: Available at local bakeries, cafes, and traditional eateries throughout the island.
- **Price**:
  - Bougatsa: €2 to €4.
  - Skiathos Cheese Pie: €3 to €6.
- **Description**:
  Skiathos offers its own unique pastries, with bougatsa and cheese pie being popular choices. Bougatsa is a sweet or savory pastry filled with custard, cream cheese, or minced meat. Skiathos cheese pie (Skiathos Bougatsa) is a local favorite that features a savory filling of locally produced cheese wrapped in flaky pastry.
- **Key Features**:
  - Enjoy as a breakfast snack or afternoon treat with a coffee.
  - Locally made, so always fresh and full of flavor.

5. Tzatziki

- **Location**: Found at most Greek restaurants and tavernas.
- **Price**: €3 to €5 per serving.

- **Description**:
  Tzatziki is one of Greece's most famous dips, made from Greek yogurt, cucumbers, garlic, and olive oil. It's a refreshing side dish that complements nearly every meal in Greece, particularly grilled meats and vegetables.
- **Key Features**:
  - Cooling and creamy, perfect for counteracting the heat of grilled dishes.
  - Often served with warm pita bread or as part of a mezze platter.

6. Horiatiki Salad (Greek Salad)

- **Location**: Most restaurants and tavernas serve this refreshing salad.
- **Price**: €6 to €10.
- **Description**:
  A classic Greek dish, the Horiatiki salad is composed of ripe tomatoes, cucumbers, red onions, olives, green peppers, and feta cheese, dressed in olive oil, oregano, and vinegar. It's simple, healthy, and incredibly flavorful, making it the perfect accompaniment to any meal.
- **Key Features**:
  - A great option for a light meal or side dish.
  - Fresh and packed with Mediterranean flavors.

7. Saganaki (Fried Cheese)

- **Location**: Available at many tavernas and traditional Greek eateries.
- **Price**: €6 to €10.
- **Description**:
  Saganaki is a delicious Greek appetizer that features cheese (often kefalograviera or feta) fried until golden and crispy. It is typically served with a squeeze of lemon and a side of pita bread.
- **Key Features**:
  - Rich, crispy, and savory, it's the ideal starter before a main course.
  - Best enjoyed with a refreshing drink, like ouzo or tsipouro.

8. Loukoumades (Greek Honey Donuts)

- **Location**: Found in local dessert shops and cafes.
- **Price**: €4 to €6.
- **Description**:
  Loukoumades are small, deep-fried dough balls that are drenched in honey syrup and sprinkled with cinnamon and crushed walnuts. These sweet treats are a popular dessert in Skiathos, offering a warm and indulgent end to any meal.

- **Key Features**:
  - Sweet, crunchy, and gooey – a perfect Greek dessert.
  - Best enjoyed warm, straight from the fryer.

Where to Enjoy Traditional Greek Cuisine in Skiathos

- **Tavernas by the Beach**: Many beachside tavernas serve a variety of traditional dishes, with seafood being a popular option. You can enjoy your meal while looking out at the crystal-clear waters of Skiathos.
- **Skiathos Town**: The town is full of tavernas, cafes, and restaurants offering both modern and traditional Greek dishes. Look for family-run establishments for an authentic experience.
- **Villas and Agrotourism**: For a truly local experience, visit one of Skiathos' agritourism spots or villages. Some offer homemade food made from ingredients sourced directly from their farms.

Greek cuisine in Skiathos is a blend of fresh, local ingredients, traditional cooking techniques, and flavors that have been perfected over centuries. From savory dishes like souvlaki and moussaka to sweet treats like loukoumades, there's no shortage of delicious food to try. Whether dining at a seaside taverna or enjoying a quiet meal in a charming village, Skiathos offers a memorable culinary experience that's not to be missed.

6.2 Best Restaurants and Cafes in Skiathos

Skiathos is home to a diverse selection of eateries, ranging from casual cafés serving fresh pastries to fine dining restaurants offering gourmet experiences. The island's culinary scene thrives on local ingredients, offering a mix of traditional Greek dishes, Mediterranean flavors, and international influences. Here's a guide to some of the best restaurants and cafés you should visit during your stay in Skiathos.

1. Taverna Muses

- **Location**: Skiathos Town, Old Harbour
- **Price**: €15 to €30 per person (main course)
- **Contact**: +30 2427 022737
- **Website**: tavernamuses.gr
- **Opening Hours**:
  - Monday to Sunday: 12:00 PM - 11:00 PM
- **Description**:
  Taverna Muses is an iconic family-run restaurant known for its warm

atmosphere and traditional Greek dishes. Located at the Old Harbour of Skiathos Town, the taverna offers stunning views of the sea while serving fresh seafood, moussaka, and local specialties like Skiathos-style octopus. Guests rave about the homemade tzatziki and the friendly, welcoming service.

- **Key Features**:
  - Fresh seafood and traditional Greek dishes.
  - Seafront dining with beautiful views.
  - homemade desserts.
- **Visitor Services**:
  - Takeaway options available.
  - Vegetarian and vegan-friendly menu.

2. Kivo Art & Gourmet Hotel Restaurant

- **Location**: Kivo Art & Gourmet Hotel, Vasilias Beach
- **Price**: €30 to €50 per person (main course)
- **Contact**: +30 2427 022558
- **Website**: kivohotel.com
- **Opening Hours**:
  - Monday to Sunday: 7:00 PM - 11:00 PM
- **Description**:

  This elegant gourmet restaurant is part of the Kivo Art & Gourmet Hotel and offers a fine dining experience with a modern twist on Greek and Mediterranean cuisine. Located by Vasilias Beach, the restaurant combines world-class flavors with an art gallery atmosphere. It's perfect for a romantic evening, with dishes like lamb shank slow-cooked .
- **Key Features**:
  - Fine dining with a focus on Mediterranean flavors.
  - Romantic ambiance with contemporary art.
  - Large selection of local cocktails.
- **Visitor Services**:
  - Reservation recommended.
  - Vegetarian and gluten-free options available.

3. The Windmill Restaurant

- **Location**: Skiathos Town, close to the Old Town Windmill
- **Price**: €20 to €40 per person (main course)
- **Contact**: +30 2427 023151
- **Website**: windmillrestaurant.gr
- **Opening Hours**:

- ○ Monday to Sunday: 1:00 PM - 10:00 PM
- **Description**:

  Located near one of the most iconic landmarks of Skiathos, The Windmill Restaurant offers stunning panoramic views of the town and the sea. It's a great place to enjoy fresh local seafood, grilled meats, and traditional Greek recipes. Known for its intimate atmosphere, it's ideal for a leisurely lunch or a romantic dinner.
- **Key Features**:
  - ○ Panoramic views of Skiathos Town and the sea.
  - ○ Focus on fresh seafood and Greek delicacies.
  - ○ Romantic and peaceful atmosphere.
- **Visitor Services**:
  - ○ Outdoor seating available with views.

4. La Bussola

- **Location**: Skiathos Town, on the waterfront near the port
- **Price**: €10 to €25 per person (main course)
- **Contact**: +30 2427 024727
- **Website**: N/A
- **Opening Hours**:
  - ○ Monday to Sunday: 12:00 PM - 10:00 PM
- **Description**:

  La Bussola is a cozy, family-friendly restaurant located near the port in Skiathos Town. Known for its authentic Italian and Mediterranean cuisine, it's perfect for those craving a taste of Italy while in Greece. The restaurant's signature dish is the seafood pasta, prepared with freshly caught fish and homemade pasta. A great spot for a casual yet delicious meal with a view of the harbor.
- **Key Features**:
  - ○ A mix of Italian and Mediterranean cuisine.
  - ○ Cozy and casual waterfront setting.
  - ○ Freshly made pasta and pizza options.
- **Visitor Services**:
  - ○ Takeout available.
  - ○ Vegetarian and gluten-free options available.

5. Agnadio Restaurant

- **Location**: Skiathos Town, near the main road
- **Price**: €12 to €20 per person (main course)
- **Contact**: +30 2427 022772

- **Website**: N/A
- **Opening Hours**:
  - Monday to Sunday: 12:30 PM - 11:00 PM
- **Description**:

  Agnadio is a popular taverna located slightly off the beaten path in Skiathos Town. This family-run restaurant offers a blend of traditional Greek dishes and Mediterranean flavors, with an emphasis on locally sourced ingredients. Guests love the grilled meats, particularly the lamb chops and souvlaki, as well as the fresh local salads and fish.

- **Key Features**:
  - Traditional Greek cooking with fresh, local ingredients.
  - Relaxed and friendly atmosphere.
  - A wide variety of meat and seafood options.
- **Visitor Services**:
  - Indoor and outdoor seating.
  - Family-friendly and child-friendly menu.

6. Bourtzi Café Bar

- **Location**: Bourtzi Peninsula, Skiathos Town
- **Price**: €4 to €10 for coffee/desserts
- **Contact**: +30 2427 023222
- **Website**: N/A
- **Opening Hours**:
  - Monday to Sunday: 9:00 AM - 12:00 AM
- **Description**:

  Located on the picturesque Bourtzi Peninsula, Bourtzi Café Bar offers breathtaking views of the sea and Skiathos Town. It's a perfect spot for enjoying a leisurely coffee or a light meal, such as pastries, sandwiches, or a refreshing Greek yogurt parfait. With its relaxed vibe, this café is great for unwinding after a day of sightseeing.

- **Key Features**:
  - Great views of the harbor and town.
  - Ideal for coffee, cocktails, and desserts.
  - Beautiful outdoor seating area by the water.
- **Visitor Services**:
  - Live music on some evenings.
  - Free Wi-Fi available for customers.

7. Katerina's Restaurant

- **Location**: Skiathos Town, near the marina
- **Price**: €12 to €25 per person (main course)
- **Contact**: +30 2427 022330
- **Website**: katerinasrestaurant.gr
- **Opening Hours**:
  - Monday to Sunday: 1:00 PM - 11:00 PM
- **Description**:
  Katerina's Restaurant is a charming family-run eatery offering traditional Greek cuisine in a cozy setting. The restaurant's specialty is the seafood platter, which features a variety of fresh fish and shellfish. Guests also rave about the quality of the moussaka and lamb dishes.
- **Key Features**:
  - Traditional Greek dishes with a focus on seafood.
  - Relaxed, welcoming environment.
- **Visitor Services**:
  - Vegetarian-friendly menu.
  - Outdoor seating available.

Skiathos offers an incredible selection of restaurants and cafés, each serving up authentic Greek flavors and Mediterranean delicacies. Whether you're looking for a fine-dining experience with views, a cozy taverna for a traditional meal, or a café for coffee and dessert by the sea, Skiathos' culinary scene has something to satisfy every taste. Be sure to explore the island's restaurants for a true taste of Greek hospitality and local flavors.

6.3 Beachside Dining and Bars in Skiathos

Skiathos, with its stunning beaches and crystal-clear waters, offers a variety of beachside dining and bar options that allow you to savor delicious food and refreshing drinks while enjoying the beautiful seaside atmosphere. From laid-back beach bars serving cocktails to upscale seafood restaurants with panoramic views, here's a guide to the best beachside spots in Skiathos.

1. Kassandra Bay Resort & Spa Beach Bar

- **Location**: Kassandra Bay Resort, Vasilias Beach
- **Price**: €8 to €20 per person (drinks and snacks)
- **Contact**: +30 2427 022200
- **Website**: kassandrabay.gr
- **Opening Hours**:

- Monday to Sunday: 9:00 AM - 11:00 PM
- **Description**:

  Nestled along Vasilias Beach, Kassandra Bay Resort & Spa's beach bar offers a luxurious yet relaxed atmosphere with a selection of cocktails, light bites, and fresh juices. Whether you're lounging by the pool or enjoying the sand, this beach bar provides the perfect place to relax after a swim or sunbathe. The beach bar is also known for its variety of refreshing cocktails made with local ingredients.
- **Key Features**:
  - Stunning views of Vasilias Beach and the Aegean Sea.
  - Cocktails, light snacks, and refreshing drinks.
  - Luxurious, tranquil ambiance perfect for relaxation.
- **Visitor Services**:
  - Lounge chairs and umbrellas available.
  - Pool access for guests.
  - Free Wi-Fi available.

2. Agia Eleni Beach Bar

- **Location**: Agia Eleni Beach
- **Price**: €5 to €15 per person (drinks and snacks)
- **Contact**: +30 2427 024548
- **Website**: N/A
- **Opening Hours**:
  - Monday to Sunday: 10:00 AM - 8:00 PM
- **Description**:

  Agia Eleni Beach Bar is a vibrant spot located on one of Skiathos' most beautiful and tranquil beaches. Known for its lively atmosphere, this bar serves a variety of tropical cocktails, iced coffees, and beach snacks like Greek salads and fresh fruit platters. The bar is perfect for those who want to enjoy a drink with their toes in the sand and is often frequented by locals and visitors alike.
- **Key Features**:
  - Cozy beachside location with views of the sea.
  - Variety of cocktails, snacks, and refreshing drinks.
  - Friendly service and great music to set the mood.
- **Visitor Services**:
  - Sunbeds and umbrellas available for rent.
  - Music and DJs on some evenings.
  - Accessible by foot from the beach.

3. Platanias Beach Restaurant and Bar

- **Location**: Platanias Beach
- **Price**: €12 to €25 per person (lunch or dinner)
- **Contact**: +30 2427 022100
- **Website**: plataniasbeach.gr
- **Opening Hours**:
  - Monday to Sunday: 12:00 PM - 11:00 PM
- **Description**:
  Situated directly on the popular Platanias Beach, this beach restaurant offers a laid-back environment with stunning views of the sea. The menu is a blend of Mediterranean and Greek cuisine, offering a wide range of seafood dishes, grilled meats, and fresh salads. Guests love the fresh fish and the relaxed dining experience with their feet in the sand.
- **Key Features**:
  - Fresh seafood and Mediterranean dishes.
  - Beachside dining with beautiful sea views.
  - Relaxed and welcoming atmosphere.
- **Visitor Services**:
  - Sunbeds and beach umbrellas available for rent.
  - Family-friendly dining with a kids' menu.
  - Special events and live music during summer.

4. Squirrel Beach Bar

- **Location**: Kolios Beach
- **Price**: €6 to €18 per person (drinks and light meals)
- **Contact**: +30 2427 024507
- **Website**: N/A
- **Opening Hours**:
  - Monday to Sunday: 9:00 AM - 10:00 PM
- **Description**:
  The Squirrel Beach Bar is a hidden gem tucked away on Kolios Beach, offering a more intimate and peaceful beachside experience. It is famous for its laid-back atmosphere, great selection of cocktails, and refreshing smoothies. The menu includes Greek-inspired tapas and light snacks, perfect for a midday bite by the sea. This bar has become a popular hangout for those seeking a calm place to enjoy the beautiful beach without the crowds.
- **Key Features**:
  - Intimate and relaxed beachside setting.
  - Light bites, tapas, and cocktails.

- o Quiet ambiance perfect for unwinding.
- **Visitor Services**:
  - o Loungers and beach beds for rent.
  - o Free Wi-Fi access.
  - o Special events and live music during peak season.

5. Vromolimnos Beach Bar

- **Location**: Vromolimnos Beach
- **Price**: €5 to €20 per person (drinks and snacks)
- **Contact**: +30 2427 027888
- **Website**: N/A
- **Opening Hours**:
  - o Monday to Sunday: 9:00 AM - 10:00 PM
- **Description**:

Vromolimnos Beach Bar is a lively and popular spot on one of Skiathos' most picturesque beaches. It offers a great selection of cocktails, iced coffees, and classic beach snacks like fries, sandwiches, and fresh fruit. The bar's energetic vibe is matched by great beach tunes, making it a perfect spot for enjoying a drink and watching the sunset over the Aegean Sea.

- **Key Features**:
  - o Fun and lively atmosphere with beach music.
  - o A wide selection of drinks and snacks.
  - o Located on one of the most beautiful and sandy beaches on the island.
- **Visitor Services**:
  - o Loungers and umbrellas available for rent.
  - o Watersports activities available at the beach.
  - o Parking area close by.

6. Elia Beach Bar

- **Location**: Elia Beach
- **Price**: €6 to €15 per person (drinks and snacks)
- **Contact**: +30 2427 024243
- **Website**: N/A
- **Opening Hours**:
  - o Monday to Sunday: 10:00 AM - 8:00 PM
- **Description**:

Elia Beach Bar is located on the secluded Elia Beach, offering a serene and laid-back vibe with incredible views of the sea. Known for its fresh fruit cocktails and a variety of snacks, this spot is perfect for those seeking a quieter place to enjoy the beach. The bar is ideal for sunbathing and sipping a cocktail while taking in the surrounding beauty.

- **Key Features**:
  - Quiet and peaceful location for a relaxed beach experience.
  - A variety of fresh fruit cocktails and light snacks.
  - Ideal for a more secluded, tranquil experience.
- **Visitor Services**:
  - Beach chairs and umbrellas available for rent.
  - Light snacks and cocktails served all day.
  - Family-friendly environment.

Beachside dining and bars in Skiathos offer a unique way to experience the island's beauty while enjoying delicious food and refreshing drinks. Whether you're looking to relax with a cocktail by the sea, enjoy fresh seafood with a view, or experience the lively atmosphere of a popular beach bar, Skiathos has something for every taste. These beachside spots allow you to immerse yourself in the natural beauty of the island while savoring the flavors of the Aegean.

6.4 Nightlife and Entertainment in Skiathos

Skiathos is renowned for its vibrant nightlife, offering an eclectic mix of clubs, bars, and venues for live music. Whether you're looking to dance the night away, enjoy a cocktail with a view, or listen to live performances, Skiathos has something to suit every mood. From energetic nightclubs to more intimate settings with live music, here's a guide to the island's best nightlife spots.

1. La Luna Bar & Club

- **Location**: Skiathos Town, 1st Floor, Papadiamantis Street
- **Price**: €8 to €18 per person (drinks and entry fees)
- **Contact**: +30 2427 022351
- **Website**: lalunaskiathos.gr
- **Opening Hours**:
  - Monday to Sunday: 10:00 PM - 4:00 AM
- **Description**:
  La Luna is one of the most famous nightlife spots in Skiathos, known for its energetic vibe and fantastic selection of cocktails. The club hosts regular DJ nights, and its spacious dance floor invites partygoers to dance until the early hours. The modern interior, coupled with cutting-edge sound and lighting systems, makes it one of the best places to experience Skiathos' vibrant nightlife scene.

- **Key Features**:
  - Large dance floor with state-of-the-art sound and lighting.
  - International DJs and live music nights.
  - Premium cocktails and extensive drink menu.
- **Visitor Services**:
  - VIP tables available for reservation.
  - Private events and themed parties.
  - Free Wi-Fi for guests.

2. Bourtzi Bar

- **Location**: Skiathos Town, Bourtzi Peninsula
- **Price**: €7 to €15 per person (drinks)
- **Contact**: +30 2427 022290
- **Website**: N/A
- **Opening Hours**:
  - Monday to Sunday: 7:00 PM - 2:00 AM
- **Description**:

  Bourtzi Bar is a unique venue set on the Bourtzi Peninsula, offering breathtaking views of the sea and the Skiathos Town harbor. Known for its relaxing atmosphere, this bar specializes in signature cocktails . It's a fantastic place to start the evening with a sunset drink or to enjoy a casual evening out with friends. The venue also hosts live acoustic sessions, making it a perfect spot for music lovers.
- **Key Features**:
  - Scenic location overlooking Skiathos Town and the harbor.
  - Signature cocktails and creative drinks menu.
  - Live acoustic performances and relaxing ambiance.
- **Visitor Services**:
  - Outdoor seating with fantastic views.
  - Light snacks and tapas available.
  - Ideal for sunset views and casual nights out.

3. 7 Sins Bar

- **Location**: Skiathos Town, Papadiamantis Street
- **Price**: €5 to €12 per person (drinks)
- **Contact**: +30 2427 024474
- **Website**: 7sins.gr
- **Opening Hours**:
  - Monday to Sunday: 9:00 PM - 3:00 AM

- **Description**:

  7 Sins Bar is one of Skiathos' trendiest spots, attracting both locals and tourists with its chic interior, specialty cocktails, and lively atmosphere. The bar often hosts themed nights and parties, with live music and performances adding to the fun. With its intimate yet energetic vibe, 7 Sins is perfect for those who enjoy a sophisticated, upbeat night out.

- **Key Features**:
  - Stylish interior with a cool, modern atmosphere.
  - Wide selection of cocktails .
  - Regular themed parties and live music events.

- **Visitor Services**:
  - VIP table reservations available.
  - Cocktail masterclasses and private events.
  - Welcoming staff and great service.

4. Skiathos Club

- **Location**: Skiathos Town, Off Papadiamantis Street
- **Price**: €10 to €20 per person (drinks and entry fees)
- **Contact**: +30 2427 022240
- **Website**: skiathosclub.gr
- **Opening Hours**:
  - Monday to Sunday: 11:00 PM - 5:00 AM
- **Description**:

  Skiathos Club is a stylish nightclub that has been a staple of the island's nightlife for years. Known for its electric atmosphere, the club hosts a mix of live performances, DJ nights, and themed parties, making it one of the best places on the island to dance the night away. The club's modern design, coupled with top-notch sound systems and special effects, creates an immersive experience for party lovers.

- **Key Features**:
  - Modern nightclub with a vibrant dance floor.
  - Regular live DJ performances and events.
  - High-quality sound and lighting effects.

- **Visitor Services**:
  - Table reservations for VIP guests.
  - Exclusive events and private parties.
  - Cocktail menu with premium drinks.

5. The Windmill Bar

- **Location**: Skiathos Town, Near the Old Port
- **Price**: €6 to €12 per person (drinks)
- **Contact**: +30 2427 022758
- **Website**: N/A
- **Opening Hours**:
  - Monday to Sunday: 7:00 PM - 2:00 AM
- **Description**:

  The Windmill Bar is a charming and quirky spot located in the heart of Skiathos Town, offering fantastic views of the harbor and a laid-back atmosphere. This bar is known for its unique setting—housed in an old windmill—and its range of refreshing cocktails and tapas. The Windmill Bar is perfect for a relaxed evening out, where you can enjoy good drinks and listen to some chill tunes. It's especially popular for its sunset views, making it a must-visit for a laid-back but scenic evening.

- **Key Features**:
  - Located in an iconic windmill building with panoramic views.
  - Cozy ambiance with chill-out music and sunset views.
  - Variety of cocktails, and light bites.
- **Visitor Services**:
  - Outdoor seating with sea views.
  - Great for watching the sunset.
  - Light snacks and tapas menu.

6. Pasha Club

- **Location**: Skiathos Town, On the Main Street
- **Price**: €10 to €25 per person (drinks and entry fees)
- **Contact**: +30 2427 022540
- **Website**: pashaclub.gr
- **Opening Hours**:
  - Monday to Sunday: 11:00 PM - 4:00 AM
- **Description**:

  Pasha Club is one of the largest and most luxurious nightclubs in Skiathos. With its modern design, high-energy dance floor, and world-class DJ performances, it's the ultimate destination for those looking to party hard in style. The club offers a wide range of drinks, including premium cocktails and champagnes, and is the place to be for those who enjoy a glamorous, high-energy nightlife scene.

- **Key Features**:
  - Exclusive nightclub with a premium atmosphere.

- Regular performances by international DJs.
- VIP services and private sections for special guests.
- **Visitor Services**:
  - VIP reservations and bottle service.
  - Exclusive events, such as private parties and themed nights.
  - High-end drinks menu and personalized services.

Skiathos nightlife offers a wide range of experiences, from chic bars offering breathtaking views to high-energy nightclubs where you can dance the night away. Whether you're seeking a relaxing evening with cocktails or an exciting night filled with live music and dancing, Skiathos is sure to provide unforgettable moments for all kinds of party-goers. Don't miss the chance to experience the lively and varied nightlife of this beautiful Greek island.

Chapter 7. Practical Travel Information

7.1 Currency and Payments in Skiathos

Skiathos, like the rest of Greece, operates on the Euro (€) as its official currency. While cash is still widely used, especially for small transactions or in more rural areas, most establishments also accept major credit and debit cards. Here's everything you need to know about currency, payments, and how to manage your finances during your visit to Skiathos.

1. Currency: Euro (€)

- **Symbol**: €
- **Notes**: €5, €10, €20, €50, €100, €200, €500
- **Coins**: 1c, 2c, 5c, 10c, 20c, 50c, €1, €2
- **Exchange Rates**:
  - Exchange rates fluctuate, so it's a good idea to check the current rate before you travel. You can also exchange currency at airports or exchange bureaus on the island. Keep in mind that exchange rates at the airport or exchange shops in tourist areas may not be as favorable as those found in the local banks.

2. ATMs and Cash Withdrawals

- **Availability**:
  - There are numerous ATMs scattered across Skiathos, particularly in the main town (Skiathos Town). You'll find ATMs at the airport, the port, and central locations around the island.
- **Fees**:
  - Be aware that many ATMs on the island charge a small withdrawal fee (usually around €2–€3 per transaction), and international banks may also charge a fee for withdrawing cash abroad.
- **Cash Withdrawal Limit**:
  - Some ATMs may have withdrawal limits, typically ranging between €200 and €500 per transaction. If you need more cash, you may need to withdraw multiple times.

3. Credit and Debit Cards

- **Accepted Cards**:
  - ○ Most hotels, restaurants, shops, and bars in Skiathos accept major credit and debit cards (Visa, MasterCard, American Express, and sometimes Maestro). However, small businesses and some rural tavernas might only accept cash.
- **Tips for Card Use**:
  - ○ Always check with the establishment beforehand to confirm they accept card payments.
  - ○ If you are using a credit or debit card abroad, notify your bank before your trip to avoid any issues with your card being blocked for suspicious activity.
  - ○ Some places may apply a surcharge (around 1% to 3%) for card payments, especially for small transactions.

4. Currency Exchange

- **Where to Exchange**:
  - ○ You can exchange currency at local banks, exchange bureaus in the town, or at the airport.
  - ○ There are also exchange offices in Skiathos Town, which offer competitive rates for exchanging foreign currency. However, they tend to have limited hours, so it's a good idea to exchange money in advance if possible.
- **Banking Hours**:
  - ○ Most banks are open from Monday to Friday, typically from 8:00 AM to 3:00 PM, though they may close earlier during the summer months. Banks are generally closed on weekends and public holidays.

5. Tipping in Skiathos

- **Customary Tipping**:
  - ○ Tipping is common in Skiathos and throughout Greece but not mandatory. It is generally appreciated for good service. Here are some tipping guidelines:
    - **Restaurants**: 5% to 10% of the bill, unless service is included in the price.
    - **Taxis**: Round up the fare or add a small tip (about 5–10%).
    - **Hotel Staff**: €1–€2 per day for housekeeping, and €5–€10 for bellhops or concierge services.
    - **Tour Guides**: €5–€10 per person for a half-day tour and €10–€20 for a full-day tour.

6. Managing Money While Traveling

- **Money Exchange Apps**:
  - You can also use money exchange apps such as Revolut, TransferWise, or PayPal to transfer money internationally at favorable rates. These apps often allow you to use your phone to pay directly or withdraw cash from ATMs with minimal fees.
- **Currency Converter Apps**:
  - Currency converter apps (like XE Currency or Revolut) can be handy to track exchange rates, ensuring you're getting the best deal when withdrawing or exchanging money.

7. Safety Tips for Handling Money

- **Keep Money Secure**:
  - Always store your cash, cards, and important documents in a safe place, such as a hotel safe or a money belt.
  - When withdrawing cash from ATMs, be aware of your surroundings, and avoid withdrawing large amounts late at night.
- **Notify Your Bank of Travel Plans**:
  - Let your bank know you will be traveling abroad to prevent any issues with card usage or fraud protection.
  - Keep a backup payment method (such as a second card) in case of loss or theft.

Managing currency and payments in Skiathos is relatively easy, with widespread availability of ATMs and the acceptance of credit and debit cards at most businesses. While cash is still important, especially for smaller transactions or in rural areas, you'll find that Skiathos is well-equipped to cater to international visitors in terms of banking and payments. To ensure a smooth trip, it's recommended to keep a small amount of local currency for emergencies while relying on cards for larger transactions.

7.2 Language and Communication in Skiathos

Skiathos, like the rest of Greece, primarily speaks Greek. However, due to its status as a popular tourist destination, English is widely understood, especially in tourist areas. Here's a guide to language and communication while visiting the island.

1. Official Language: Greek

- **Language Family**: Greek belongs to the Indo-European language family, with a unique alphabet and rich history dating back thousands of years.

- **Alphabets**: Greek uses the Greek alphabet, which can be a bit challenging for non-Greek speakers. However, most signs in Skiathos, especially in tourist spots, are bilingual, featuring both Greek and English.

- **Common Phrases**: While English is widely spoken, learning a few basic Greek phrases can enrich your experience and show respect for the local culture. Here are some useful Greek phrases:

  - **Hello** – Χαίρετε (Cheretete) or Γειά σας (Yia sas)
  - **Goodbye** – Αντίο (Adio)
  - **Thank you** – Ευχαριστώ (Efharisto)
  - **Please** – Παρακαλώ (Parakalo)
  - **Yes** – Ναι (Ne)
  - **No** – Όχι (Ochi)
  - **How much does this cost?** – Πόσο κοστίζει αυτό; (Poso kostizei afto?)
  - **Where is the bathroom?** – Που είναι η τουαλέτα; (Pou einai i toualeta?)
  - **I don't speak Greek** – Δεν μιλάω Ελληνικά (Den milao Ellinika)

2. English Proficiency

- **Widespread Usage**:
  - English is commonly spoken in Skiathos, especially in hotels, restaurants, shops, and tourist attractions. Staff members in most service-oriented industries, including taxi drivers and tour operators, generally speak English to a conversational level.
- **In More Remote Areas**:
  - In less touristy areas or in more traditional settings, you may find fewer people who speak English fluently. In such cases, a smile, patience, and some basic Greek words can help. Learning a few simple phrases can go a long way in making a positive impression.

3. Communication Tools

- **Wi-Fi Access**:

  - Wi-Fi is widely available in hotels, restaurants, cafes, and even some public spaces in Skiathos Town and other popular tourist spots. While some places offer free Wi-Fi, others may charge a small fee for access.
  - Many places in Skiathos offer high-speed internet, but be aware that in more remote parts of the island, the connection might be slower or less reliable.

- **Local SIM Cards and Data Plans**:

  - If you're planning on using your phone extensively while in Skiathos, consider purchasing a local SIM card for data and calls.

  - Greek mobile carriers, such as Cosmote, Vodafone Greece, and Wind, offer prepaid SIM cards with data plans at affordable prices. These are available at kiosks, convenience stores, or mobile shops around Skiathos Town.

  - **SIM Card Requirements**:

    - To purchase a SIM card, you'll need to show your passport or ID, and some carriers may require proof of address (such as your hotel booking).
    - Coverage on the island is generally good, but remote areas and certain beaches may have limited reception.

4. Emergency Communication

- **Emergency Numbers**:
  - **Police**: 100
  - **Fire Department**: 199
  - **Ambulance**: 166
  - **Tourist Police**: 171
- **Medical Services**:
  - Skiathos has a well-equipped hospital (Skiathos General Hospital) in the town, as well as several pharmacies throughout the island. In case of minor health issues or emergencies, you can seek assistance from these places.

5. Post and Communication Services

- **Post Offices**:

  - Skiathos has a central post office located in Skiathos Town, offering services like mail, parcels, and postal banking. The address for the main post office is:
    - **Skiathos Post Office**
    - **Location**: Skiathos Town, Papadiamantis Street, near the Old Port.
    - **Opening Hours**: Monday to Friday: 8:00 AM - 2:30 PM, Closed on Saturdays and Sundays.
- **Phone Booths and Postal Services**:

  - Public phone booths are available in certain areas of Skiathos Town, but they are becoming less common due to the widespread use of mobile phones.
  - You can also send postcards, letters, and packages at the post office.

6. Communication Etiquette

- **Polite Conversation**:
  - Greeks are known for their hospitality and warmth. It's considered polite to greet people with a smile and show respect by addressing older individuals or locals with titles like "Kalimera" (Good morning) or "Kalispera" (Good evening) and using "Parakalo" (Please) and "Efharisto" (Thank you).
- **Body Language**:
  - Body language in Greece tends to be expressive, and Greeks use their hands when speaking. This can be helpful to understand certain points in a conversation, especially when there are language barriers.

While Greek is the official language of Skiathos, the island is a popular destination with many locals and businesses fluent in English, especially in the tourist areas. Visitors should have little trouble communicating, although learning a few key Greek phrases can enhance the travel experience and help build a positive rapport with locals. Additionally, modern communication tools such as Wi-Fi, local SIM cards, and online translation apps can easily bridge any language gaps, ensuring that visitors have a smooth and enjoyable stay on the island.

7.3 Safety and Health in Skiathos

Skiathos is a safe and welcoming destination for travelers, with a well-established healthcare system and reliable emergency services. However, like any international destination, it's important to be aware of local safety tips and health precautions. This section will guide you through essential safety and health information for your trip to Skiathos, including emergency contacts, healthcare services, and travel insurance.

1. Safety Tips

- **General Safety**:
  - Skiathos is generally considered a very safe destination, with a low crime rate. Petty crimes such as pickpocketing can occasionally occur in crowded tourist areas, so it's recommended to keep an eye on your personal belongings, especially in busy spots like Skiathos Town and beaches.
- **Personal Safety**:
  - When walking or hiking, be mindful of the uneven terrain, especially in remote or less developed areas. Sturdy footwear is advisable for hiking trails and exploring the island's natural beauty.
  - Always stay hydrated and wear sunscreen to avoid sunburns, as Skiathos can get very hot during the summer months.
- **Swimming Safety**:
  - Skiathos has some rocky beaches and areas with strong currents. While most beaches have lifeguards, it's always important to pay attention to local warnings or flags indicating swimming conditions.
- **Wildlife**:
  - Skiathos is home to some wildlife, including seabirds and small reptiles. However, dangerous animals are rare. When hiking, be cautious of snakes in forested areas, although bites are infrequent.

2. Emergency Contacts

- **Emergency Numbers**:

  - **Police**: 100
  - **Fire Department**: 199
  - **Ambulance**: 166
  - **Tourist Police**: 171
  - **Skiathos General Hospital (for medical emergencies)**: +30 24270 22222
  - **Coast Guard**: +30 24270 22166

- **Local Hospitals**:

  - **Skiathos General Hospital** is the main medical facility on the island, providing emergency care, basic medical services, and diagnostic testing. In more severe cases, patients may need to be transferred to mainland Greece.

  - **Address**: Skiathos Town, Vasilias area, Skiathos, Greece.

  - **Opening Hours**: The hospital is open 24/7 for emergencies.

- **Pharmacies**:

  - There are several pharmacies throughout the island, particularly in Skiathos Town, where you can obtain over-the-counter medication or seek advice for minor health issues. Pharmacy staff typically speak English.
  - **Pharmacy Locations**: Most pharmacies are in Skiathos Town, with a few in more rural areas.
  - **Opening Hours**: Most pharmacies operate Monday to Friday, 8:00 AM to 2:30 PM, with a break in the afternoon. Some also open for a few hours on Saturdays.

3. Healthcare Services

- **Public Healthcare**:

  - Greece has a robust public healthcare system that is available to all residents and visitors. Skiathos has a well-equipped hospital and several private healthcare providers catering to tourists. However, most healthcare facilities on the island focus on basic medical care. In case of more complex health issues, patients may need to be transferred to a larger hospital on the mainland.
- **Private Healthcare Providers**:

  - **Skiathos Medical Center** offers private medical services and is located in the heart of Skiathos Town. They can handle general consultations, minor injuries, and provide medical advice.

  - **Contact**: +30 24270 26017

- **Medical Assistance for Tourists**:

  - Several doctors and healthcare professionals cater specifically to tourists, with some providing English-speaking services. If you require medical help while on the island, you can easily reach out to your hotel's reception or your tour operator for recommendations on where to go.

4. Travel Insurance

- **Why Travel Insurance is Important**:

  - Travel insurance is highly recommended for any trip abroad, especially to cover health-related issues, trip cancellations, lost baggage, or emergency medical transportation. Skiathos has adequate healthcare facilities, but if you need specialized medical care or evacuation to a mainland hospital, the costs can be high without insurance.

- **Coverage to Consider**:

  - **Emergency Medical Coverage**: Ensure that your travel insurance covers emergency medical expenses abroad, including medical evacuations if necessary.
  - **Trip Cancellation or Interruption**: If unforeseen circumstances force you to cancel or interrupt your trip, having this coverage can help you recover some of your travel expenses.
  - **Personal Liability**: This is useful if you accidentally cause injury or damage while on vacation.

- **Travel Insurance Providers**:

  - Popular travel insurance providers like Allianz, World Nomads, and Travel Guard offer comprehensive plans that can be customized to suit your needs. Many of these providers have 24/7 emergency assistance hotlines and can quickly help you arrange medical care or evacuation in case of an emergency.

- **How to Purchase Travel Insurance**:

  - Travel insurance can be purchased online before your trip, and it's best to do so as early as possible after booking your travel arrangements. Make sure to read the terms and conditions carefully to ensure your coverage meets your needs, especially for medical emergencies abroad.

5. Vaccinations and Health Precautions

- **Vaccinations**:

  - No specific vaccinations are required for traveling to Skiathos. However, it's always a good idea to ensure you are up to date on routine vaccinations such as measles, mumps, rubella, tetanus, and diphtheria before traveling.

- **Mosquito Protection**:

  - In the summer months, mosquitoes are common in Greece, especially around the evening. It's advisable to use insect repellent and wear long sleeves and pants in the evenings to avoid bites, particularly if you're visiting the beaches or rural areas.

- **Sun Protection**:

  - The sun can be intense in Skiathos, especially during the summer. Ensure that you have sunscreen with high SPF (30 or higher), wear a hat, and drink plenty of water to stay hydrated.

Skiathos is a safe destination, and visitors generally don't encounter significant health risks. By staying vigilant about personal safety, having access to emergency contacts, and taking common-sense precautions such as wearing sunscreen and staying hydrated, you can ensure a worry-free vacation. It's also essential to have travel insurance in place to cover unexpected medical situations or emergencies. With proper preparation, your stay in Skiathos will be safe, enjoyable, and memorable.

7.4 Local Etiquette and Customs in Skiathos

Skiathos is known for its warm and welcoming locals, who embrace both traditional Greek culture and the international visitors that come to the island. Understanding the local etiquette and customs can help you engage more meaningfully with the people and experience the island in a more authentic way. This section will guide you through the essential etiquette and customs to keep in mind when visiting Skiathos.

1. Greetings and Politeness

- **Warm Welcome**:
  - Greeks are renowned for their hospitality, and Skiathos is no exception. A friendly greeting is an important part of local culture. The typical greeting is a handshake, often accompanied by a smile. In more casual or familiar settings, a hug or cheek kiss may be common, especially among friends or close acquaintances.

- **Common Phrases**:
  - While English is widely spoken in Skiathos, it is always appreciated when visitors use some basic Greek greetings. A few polite phrases can help you connect with locals:
    - **Hello** – Χαίρετε (Cheretete) or Γειά σας (Yia sas)
    - **Good morning** – Καλημέρα (Kalimera)
    - **Good evening** – Καλησπέρα (Kalispera)
    - **Goodbye** – Αντίο (Adio)
    - **Thank you** – Ευχαριστώ (Efharisto)
    - **Please** – Παρακαλώ (Parakalo)
    - **How are you?** – Τι κάνετε; (Ti kanate?)
- **Titles and Respect**:
  - In Greece, using formal titles like "Mr." (Κύριος - Kyrie) and "Mrs." (Κυρία - Kyria) is customary, especially when addressing older people or strangers. First names are typically used for younger individuals or those you are familiar with.
  - It's polite to address people by their titles until you are invited to use their first names.

2. Dining Etiquette

- **Table Manners**:

  - Dining in Greece is an important social occasion. When dining in Skiathos, it's expected that you wait for the host to begin the meal before you start eating. If you're invited to someone's home, wait for everyone to be seated before starting.
  - **Saying "Kali Orexi"**: This is the Greek equivalent of "Enjoy your meal," and it is commonly said before you begin eating.
- **Tipping**:

  - Tipping is appreciated but not compulsory in Greece. In restaurants, it is customary to leave a tip of about 5-10% of the bill if the service was good. In cafes or smaller eateries, rounding up the bill is a common practice.
  - For taxi drivers, rounding up the fare or leaving a small tip is appreciated, though not expected.
  - Tipping hotel staff for their services (like cleaning or concierge) is not mandatory, but a small token of appreciation is always welcome.

- **Food Customs**:

  - Greek meals are typically served in a family-style manner, with dishes placed in the center of the table for everyone to share. Don't rush through the meal; Greeks enjoy a leisurely dining experience, often lasting several hours, especially during dinner.
  - **Food and Drink**: If you're invited to someone's home for dinner, it's customary to bring a small gift, such as dessert, or something local from your country.

3. Dress Code

- **Casual Yet Respectful**:
  - Skiathos is a laid-back, casual destination, so comfortable clothing is acceptable in most places, especially in tourist areas. However, when visiting religious sites such as churches and monasteries, it's essential to dress modestly. Women should avoid wearing short skirts or sleeveless tops, and men should avoid wearing shorts.
- **Beach Attire**:
  - On the beaches, swimwear is appropriate, but it is customary to cover up with a towel, sarong, or light clothing when walking around or entering restaurants and shops near the beach.
- **Evening Wear**:
  - For evenings out, particularly in more upscale restaurants, the dress code is casual but neat. It's not necessary to wear formal clothing, but it's recommended to avoid wearing beachwear or overly casual attire.

4. Religious Customs

- **Orthodox Christianity**:

  - The majority of the population in Skiathos practices Greek Orthodoxy, and religious customs play a significant role in the island's culture. It's important to show respect when visiting churches or monasteries.
  - If you visit a religious site, remember to dress modestly (covering shoulders, avoiding short skirts or shorts) and remain quiet inside. It's customary to light a candle for prayer in many churches, which is an act of respect and reverence.

- **Celebrations and Festivals**:

  - Skiathos hosts various religious festivals, especially around Orthodox holidays like Easter. During these times, you may observe local customs such as special church services, processions, and traditional meals.
  - **Panagia Skiathiotissa**: One of the island's biggest festivals, taking place on August 15, celebrating the Assumption of the Virgin Mary with processions, feasts, and fireworks.

5. Social Customs and Hospitality

- **Offering Drinks**:

  - Greeks are known for their hospitality, and it's not uncommon for locals to offer you a drink or a small snack as a sign of friendliness, even if you're just walking into a shop or a café. Refusing this hospitality may be seen as impolite, so it's often best to accept the gesture with gratitude, even if it's just a small glass of water.

- **Invitations**:

  - If you are invited to a local's home, it's considered polite to accept, even if you cannot stay for long. Greek families often take pride in their homes and will happily share their food, music, and company with visitors. Bringing a small gift.

  -

  - **Punctuality**:

  - Greeks are generally relaxed about time, and it is not unusual for gatherings to begin a little later than scheduled. However, if you're invited to dinner or an event, it's polite to arrive within 15-30 minutes of the stated time.

6. Respecting Local Traditions

- **Sustainable Tourism**:
  - As tourism is a significant part of Skiathos' economy, it's important to be respectful of the environment. Avoid littering, and be mindful of your impact on the island's natural beauty. Recycling is encouraged, and you'll often find designated bins for waste disposal and recycling in public areas.

- **Respect for Local Life**:
  - Greek island life is laid-back, and locals value their time in the evening and on Sundays. Try to respect their slower pace of life, particularly on Sundays when many businesses close in observance of the local tradition.

Skiathos has a rich and welcoming culture, and being mindful of the local etiquette and customs can greatly enhance your travel experience. Embrace the warmth and hospitality of the locals by learning a few Greek phrases, showing respect for religious traditions, and engaging with the community in a thoughtful and polite manner. By respecting the island's customs, you will not only enjoy a smoother visit but also leave a positive impression on the people you meet.

Chapter 8. Itinerary Suggestions

8.1 2-Day Itinerary for First-Time Visitors to Skiathos

Skiathos, with its mix of beautiful beaches, vibrant town life, and rich culture, offers plenty to see and do. For a first-time visitor, a short 2-day stay provides the perfect opportunity to get a taste of what the island has to offer. Here's a recommended 2-day itinerary that combines scenic views, cultural landmarks, relaxation, and a touch of adventure.

Day 1: Exploring Skiathos Town and Beaches

Morning: Discover Skiathos Town (Chora)

- **Start with a leisurely breakfast** at a café in **Skiathos Town**, the heart of the island. Try some traditional Greek pastries, such as **bougatsa** (custard-filled pastry) or **koulouri** (sesame bread ring), and enjoy a cup of Greek coffee.

- **Explore the Old Town**: Wander through the narrow, cobbled streets of **Skiathos Town**, lined with whitewashed buildings, vibrant bougainvillea, and quaint shops. The **Bourtzi Peninsula** offers great views of the town and harbor, and it's an excellent place to enjoy a peaceful morning stroll.

- **Visit the **Skiathos Archaeological Museum**: Located near the harbor, this small museum showcases the island's ancient history, including artifacts from the prehistoric, classical, and Roman periods. Admission is typically around €3, and it's open from 8:30 AM to 3:00 PM.

Lunch:

- Enjoy lunch at a **taverna** in Skiathos Town. Try local dishes like **souvlaki**, **moussaka**, and fresh seafood, accompanied by a glass of **retsina** .

- **Afternoon: Beach Time**

- **Visit Lalaria Beach**: After lunch, take a boat trip from the town's port to **Lalaria Beach**, one of the most famous beaches on the island. The beach is accessible only by boat, but its crystal-clear waters and dramatic cliffs make it well worth the visit. You'll find a mix of sunbathing, swimming, and photography opportunities.

- ○ **Tip**: Bring comfortable shoes and water, as there are no facilities on the beach.
- **Alternative Option – Visit Koukounaries Beach**: If you prefer a more accessible beach with sunbeds and beach bars, head to **Koukounaries Beach**, often considered one of the best beaches on the island. The golden sand and shallow waters make it ideal for swimming and lounging.

Evening: Dinner and Sunset

- Head back to Skiathos Town for a relaxed dinner at one of the **harborfront restaurants**. Enjoy local seafood dishes like grilled octopus or **spaghetti with seafood**, while watching the sunset over the harbor.

- After dinner, take a stroll along the harbor promenade, where you can explore some of the local shops and cafés or enjoy a drink at one of the island's bars.

Day 2: Cultural Exploration and Adventure

Morning: Visit Historical Sites and Monasteries

- **Visit the Monastery of Evangelistria**: Located a short drive or hike from Skiathos Town, this monastery is an important historical and religious site. It dates back to the 18th century and offers beautiful views of the island, as well as an opportunity to learn about the island's religious history. It is open daily from 8:00 AM to 1:00 PM, and admission is usually free or a small donation is requested.

- **Explore the Old Harbour (Kastro)**: If you're up for a more active morning, visit the **Kastro**, a historical site and medieval fortress located on a hill with stunning views over the island. It's a bit of a hike, but the panoramic views and the remnants of the old town make it well worth the effort.

Lunch:

- Have lunch at **Taverna To Steki**, a cozy spot with great local dishes, located in the area around **Koukounaries Beach**. Try **Greek salad**, **souvlaki**, or a delicious **seafood platter**.

Afternoon: Adventure and Nature

- **Hiking at Skiathos' Trails**: After lunch, explore the island's natural beauty with a short hike through one of its scenic trails. Skiathos is known for its lush pine forests and rugged coastline. Some popular routes are near **Koukounaries** or **Skiathos' Nature Reserve**.
  - **Alternative Option – Visit Skiathos' Waterfalls**: For a more relaxed outdoor experience, head to **Skiathos' Waterfalls**, which is a small, tranquil spot perfect for a nature walk and a refreshing dip in the cool waters.

Evening: Dinner and Nightlife

- Enjoy a **traditional Greek dinner** at a taverna on **Banana Beach**, an excellent location for a sunset meal. Many restaurants offer fresh seafood, local cheeses, and meze (small appetizers) that you can share with friends or family.

- **Nightlife in Skiathos Town**: After dinner, spend your evening experiencing the island's nightlife. Skiathos Town has a range of bars, clubs, and music venues. Whether you prefer a chilled-out cocktail bar with a sea view or a lively night out at a local club, Skiathos offers something for everyone.

  - **For a more laid-back evening**, visit **La Luna Bar**, which is perched on the hillside, offering panoramic views of the island.

  - **For those interested in dancing, Boomerang Club** is one of the island's most popular nightclubs, featuring international DJs and a fun atmosphere.

Additional Tips:

- **Transportation**: Rent a car, bike, or use local taxis to get around the island, as many of the top attractions and beaches are spread out.

- **Stay Hydrated**: The island can get very hot in the summer, so make sure to drink plenty of water, especially if you're out exploring during the day.

- **Book Activities in Advance**: If you plan to take boat tours, such as to Lalaria Beach or around the island, consider booking in advance to secure a spot.

In just two days, you can experience a perfect blend of Skiathos' natural beauty, cultural landmarks, and vibrant town life. From the charming streets of Skiathos Town to the tranquil beaches and historic monasteries, this itinerary provides a well-rounded introduction to the island. Whether you're relaxing by the sea, hiking through nature, or exploring its rich history, Skiathos will leave you with lasting memories.

8.2 5-Day Itinerary for Explorers in Skiathos

For those with more time to explore, a 5-day itinerary provides an excellent opportunity to discover Skiathos in greater depth, from its scenic beaches and natural beauty to its historical landmarks and unique island charm. This itinerary balances adventure, relaxation, culture, and nature, allowing visitors to experience the island's diverse offerings.

Day 1: Arrival and Skiathos Town Exploration

Morning: Arrival and Settling In

- **Arrive in Skiathos** and check into your accommodation. If you arrive early, enjoy a leisurely breakfast in **Skiathos Town** (Chora). Try a traditional Greek coffee paired with **bougatsa** (Greek custard pastry).

- **Walk through the Old Town**: Begin your exploration of Skiathos Town, wandering through its maze of narrow alleys, whitewashed houses with colorful shutters, and quaint shops. Take in the local charm and stop by the **Bourtzi Peninsula,** where you can enjoy scenic views over the harbor and the island.

Afternoon: Cultural Exploration

- **Visit the Skiathos Archaeological Museum**: Head to this small but informative museum to learn about the island's rich history, from ancient artifacts to more recent periods. The museum is located near the town center and provides insight into the island's past.

- **Explore the harbor and enjoy lunch** at one of the waterfront tavernas. Savor local dishes like **souvlaki**, **moussaka**, or fresh seafood.

Evening: Sunset Views and Dinner

- **Sunset at the Old Port**: In the late afternoon, enjoy a relaxed stroll along the old port. This area offers fantastic views, and it's a great place to enjoy the sunset. Head to **La Luna Bar** for panoramic views of the town while enjoying a drink.

- **Dinner in Skiathos Town**: Experience authentic Greek cuisine in one of the local tavernas. Choose from dishes like **grilled octopus**, **fava** (yellow split pea puree), and **Greek salad**.

Day 2: Beaches and Water Activities

Morning: Koukounaries Beach

- After breakfast, head to **Koukounaries Beach**, one of Skiathos' most famous beaches. The beach is known for its golden sand and clear, shallow waters, making it perfect for swimming and sunbathing. You can rent sunbeds and umbrellas, or just relax on the sand.

- **Try Water Sports**: Spend your morning exploring the waters with activities like **kayaking**, **windsurfing**, or **paddleboarding**. Local rental shops provide all the equipment you need for a fun-filled day.

Lunch: Beachside Dining

- Enjoy a relaxed lunch at one of the beachside restaurants near Koukounaries. Try fresh fish or a **Greek meze platter** while listening to the sound of the waves.

Afternoon: Visit Banana Beach

- After lunch, take a short walk to **Banana Beach**, another stunning spot known for its clear waters and serene atmosphere. Banana Beach offers more privacy, so it's a great option for those seeking a quieter experience.

- **Relax or Explore the Waterfalls**: You can either relax by the beach or, if you're up for a bit of adventure, hike to the nearby **Skiathos Waterfalls**, which are about a 30-minute walk away through the lush greenery.

Evening: Dinner in Skiathos Town

- Return to Skiathos Town for dinner. Choose a waterfront restaurant with views of the harbor, where you can enjoy delicious **seafood** or traditional Greek **lamb kleftiko**.

Day 3: Cultural and Historical Tour

Morning: Visit Evangelistria Monastery

- Begin your day with a visit to the **Monastery of Evangelistria**, located a short drive or hike from Skiathos Town. This monastery is an important religious site on the island, offering both historical significance and incredible views over Skiathos.

- **Learn about Local History**: Take some time to explore the monastery's museum and learn about the island's religious history, including its role in the Greek War of Independence. The monastery is open daily from 8:00 AM to 1:00 PM.

Lunch:

- Stop by **Taverna To Steki** or a similar local spot for a traditional lunch. Dishes like **souvlaki**, **gyros**, or **feta cheese in filo pastry** are local favorites.

Afternoon: Explore the Kastro Fortress

- In the afternoon, head to **Kastro**, the medieval fortress located on the northern coast of the island. The site offers a glimpse into Skiathos' history and incredible panoramic views. It's a bit of a hike, but the reward is worth it, as you'll see the remains of the old town and enjoy the breathtaking views of the Aegean.

- **Explore Kastro Village**: After touring the fortress, take a walk through the small village nearby. Enjoy the traditional Greek atmosphere and relax in one of the village's quiet spots.

Evening: Traditional Greek Dinner

- Return to Skiathos Town for dinner. Enjoy a leisurely meal of **stifado** (Greek beef stew) or **pastitsio** (Greek lasagna).

- **Day 4: Island Hopping and Boat Tours**

Morning: Boat Tour to Lalaria Beach

- Take a morning **boat tour** from Skiathos Town to **Lalaria Beach**, one of the island's most famous beaches. Known for its unique white pebbles and dramatic cliffs, Lalaria is accessible only by boat, which makes it even more special.

- **Enjoy the Beach**: Once at Lalaria, take time to swim in the crystal-clear waters and marvel at the natural beauty of the surroundings.

Lunch: Picnic on the Beach

- Many boat tours offer the option of a **picnic lunch** on Lalaria Beach. Alternatively, you can return to Skiathos Town for lunch.

Afternoon: Boat Tour to Skopelos or Skiathos' Smaller Islands

- In the afternoon, consider taking a boat trip to the neighboring island of **Skopelos**, which is famous for its lush greenery and beautiful beaches. The boat ride from Skiathos takes approximately 30 minutes.

- Explore **Skopelos Town** with its charming old town, or relax on beaches like **Stafilos** or **Velanio Beach**.

Evening: Dinner in Skiathos

- Return to Skiathos in the late afternoon. For dinner, head to a local restaurant to enjoy grilled lamb chops or **souvlaki** with a side of tzatziki and pita bread.

Day 5: Nature and Adventure

Morning: Hiking and Outdoor Exploration

- Spend your final day on the island embracing its natural beauty. Head to **Skiathos Nature Reserve**, a large, protected area where you can hike through lush pine forests and enjoy panoramic views of the island. There are several marked trails suitable for various fitness levels.

- **Visit the Monastery of Agios Nikolaos**: If you're interested in combining nature and history, visit the **Monastery of Agios Nikolaos**, located at the base of Mount Papos. It's a peaceful place surrounded by nature, perfect for some quiet reflection.

Lunch:

- Enjoy a rustic lunch at a countryside taverna, where you can try traditional island dishes such as **gemista** (stuffed vegetables) or **keftedes** (Greek meatballs).

Afternoon: Relaxing at the Beach

- After a morning of hiking and exploration, unwind with a visit to **Achladies Beach** or **Vassilias Beach**, both located near Skiathos Town. These quieter beaches are great for a more relaxed afternoon of swimming and sunbathing.

Evening: Final Sunset and Farewell Dinner

- As your trip comes to a close, enjoy one final **sunset dinner** at a restaurant overlooking the Aegean Sea. Choose a spot with views of the harbor, and enjoy the last flavors of Skiathos with fresh seafood or **Greek meze**.

- **Nightcap at a Local Bar**: End your stay with a drink at one of the vibrant bars in Skiathos Town or near the port. Whether you prefer a cocktail .

- it's the perfect way to toast your unforgettable adventure.

This 5-day itinerary offers a well-rounded experience of Skiathos, from its beautiful beaches and rich history to its charming town life and outdoor adventures. Whether you're soaking up the sun on secluded beaches, hiking through scenic trails, or diving into the island's culture, Skiathos has something for every explorer. By the end of your stay, you'll have experienced the best the island has to offer, leaving with memories to last a lifetime.

8.3 7-Day Itinerary for a Relaxing Getaway in Skiathos

For those who prefer a more laid-back, leisurely approach to exploring Skiathos, a 7-day itinerary is the perfect way to unwind, enjoy the island's natural beauty, and experience its peaceful atmosphere without feeling rushed. This itinerary focuses on relaxation, beautiful beaches, slow exploration, and indulgence in the local culture, providing the ultimate escape from the hustle and bustle of everyday life.

Day 1: Arrival and Skiathos Town Stroll

Morning: Arrival and Settling In

- **Arrive in Skiathos** and check into your accommodation, whether it's a beachside hotel, a private villa, or a cozy guesthouse.
- Start the day with a relaxing breakfast at your hotel or a café in **Skiathos Town** (Chora). Enjoy freshly brewed coffee, pastries, and some local specialties like **loukoumades** (Greek honey doughnuts).

Afternoon: Gentle Exploration of Skiathos Town

- **Wander around the Old Town**: Explore the narrow streets of Skiathos Town, lined with charming shops, cafes, and local boutiques. Stroll along the harbor, take in the picturesque views, and relax in one of the waterfront cafes.

- **Relax in Bourtzi Park**: Head to the **Bourtzi Peninsula** for a peaceful afternoon walk. The park offers lovely views over the port and is an excellent spot for unwinding.

Evening: Dinner with a View

- Enjoy a relaxing dinner at a restaurant overlooking the harbor, such as **The Windmill Restaurant**, which offers a combination of local delicacies and panoramic views.

Day 2: Beach Day at Koukounaries and Banana Beach

Morning: Koukounaries Beach

- Start your day with a **leisurely breakfast** and head to **Koukounaries Beach**, one of the island's most beautiful beaches. Spend your morning swimming in the crystal-clear waters, lounging on the soft sand, or taking a shaded nap under the trees.

Afternoon: Banana Beach

- After a morning of relaxation at Koukounaries, take a short walk or drive to **Banana Beach**. Known for its calm waters and peaceful atmosphere, Banana Beach is perfect for sunbathing and enjoying the serene surroundings.
- **Lunch at a Beach Bar**: Opt for a light lunch at a beachside bar offering Greek salads, grilled fish, and refreshing beverages.

Evening: Sunset and Dinner

- As the day winds down, head back to your accommodation and freshen up for dinner.
- **Enjoy a relaxed dinner** at a seaside taverna, such as **Taverna To Steki**, where you can sample delicious dishes like **grilled octopus** or **sea bream**.

Day 3: Visit to the Monasteries and Scenic Views

Morning: Monastery of Evangelistria

- Begin the day with a visit to **Monastery of Evangelistria**, a peaceful and historic site located inland. Enjoy the serenity of the monastery, and take in the beautiful views of the surrounding landscapes.

- **Explore the Museum**: Take a moment to explore the small museum at the monastery, which showcases religious artifacts and important pieces of the island's history.

Afternoon: Lunch and Scenic Views

- Head back to Skiathos Town and enjoy a leisurely lunch at a local taverna. Try traditional dishes like **pastitsio** (Greek lasagna) or **gemista** (stuffed vegetables).

- **Scenic Drive Around the Island**: After lunch, take a scenic drive along the coast to enjoy panoramic views of the Aegean Sea. Stop at various viewpoints for photo opportunities, and savor the tranquil beauty of Skiathos.

Evening: Dinner in Skiathos Town

- Return to Skiathos Town for dinner at **Ouzeri Loukia**, where you can enjoy a variety of small Greek plates like **tzatziki**, **dolmades** (stuffed grape leaves), and **saganaki** (fried cheese).

Day 4: Pamper Yourself with a Spa Day

Morning: Spa and Wellness

- Treat yourself to a **spa day** at one of the island's wellness centers or hotels that offer spa treatments. Choose from a range of rejuvenating services, such as a full-body massage, facial treatments, and aromatherapy.

Afternoon: Relaxation by the Pool or Beach

- After your spa treatment, spend the afternoon lounging by your hotel pool or head to a quiet beach like **Achladies Beach** for a peaceful and relaxing experience.
- Enjoy a light lunch at a beachside café with fresh salads, fruit, or seafood.

Evening: Sunset and Relaxed Dining

- Unwind with a casual **sunset cocktail** at a local beach bar, such as **Skiathos Sunset Bar**, and watch the vibrant colors of the sky as the sun sets over the Aegean.
- For dinner, opt for a **low-key meal** at **The Garden Taverna**, known for its warm ambiance and classic Greek dishes.

Day 5: Boat Trip to Lalaria Beach and Surrounding Islands

Morning: Boat Tour to Lalaria Beach

- Set sail on a **morning boat trip** from Skiathos Town to **Lalaria Beach**, known for its striking white pebbles and clear turquoise waters. This beach is only accessible by boat, so it's a perfect destination for a relaxing getaway.

- **Relax at the Beach**: Spend your morning swimming, sunbathing, and marveling at the dramatic cliffs surrounding Lalaria. Take in the tranquil atmosphere and enjoy the isolation of this stunning beach.

Afternoon: Picnic and Exploration

- Enjoy a **picnic lunch** on the beach or onboard the boat. Many boat trips offer a meal service, so you can savor a variety of Greek mezze and fresh fruits while surrounded by nature.

- If you're feeling adventurous, explore the nearby small coves and beaches accessible only by boat, such as **Kastani Beach** (featured in the movie *Mamma Mia!*).

Evening: Return to Skiathos

- After a day of sun and sea, return to Skiathos and spend the evening at leisure. You may want to enjoy a quiet dinner at **Taverna La Scala**, a local favorite known for its warm hospitality and Mediterranean dishes.

Day 6: Nature and Outdoor Exploration

Morning: Hiking and Scenic Views

- Head out early for a **nature walk** or light **hiking** in one of Skiathos' protected reserves, such as the **Skiathos Nature Reserve** or **Papadiamantis Park**. These areas offer lush green landscapes, wildlife sightings, and breathtaking views of the island.

- **Pack a Picnic**: Bring a light picnic along with you and enjoy it in a scenic spot amidst nature.

Afternoon: Beach Relaxation

- After your nature walk, head to **Vassilias Beach** for a more secluded and quiet beach experience. Spend the afternoon swimming, reading a book, or simply enjoying the calm waters.

Evening: Dinner with Local Flavor

- Enjoy a **relaxed dinner** at **Taverna Kavouras**, a local eatery known for its friendly atmosphere and hearty portions of Greek food like **souvlaki** and **stifado** (Greek beef stew).

Day 7: Final Day of Leisure and Farewell Dinner

Morning: Relax at the Beach

- Spend your final morning in Skiathos at **Achladies Beach**, one of the quieter spots on the island. Lounge under the sun, swim, and enjoy the last moments of peaceful relaxation.

Afternoon: Last-Minute Shopping and Souvenirs

- Head to Skiathos Town for some **last-minute shopping** at the local boutiques and markets. Pick up souvenirs like handmade jewelry, locally produced olive oil, and traditional Greek ceramics.

Evening: Sunset Dinner and Farewell

- For your final dinner, opt for a **romantic sunset dinner** at **Skiathos Yacht Club**, where you can enjoy gourmet cuisine while watching the sun dip below the horizon.
- Reflect on your relaxing getaway as you savor the flavors of the island one last time.

This 7-day itinerary is designed for those who wish to relax, unwind, and soak in the beauty of Skiathos without the rush of a typical tourist schedule. Whether you're lounging on idyllic beaches, enjoying scenic hikes, or indulging in the island's culinary delights, Skiathos offers the perfect setting for a peaceful and rejuvenating vacation. By the end of your stay, you'll leave feeling refreshed, with lasting memories of this enchanting Greek island.

8.4 Family-Friendly Itinerary in Skiathos

Skiathos is an excellent destination for families, offering a combination of relaxed beaches, scenic beauty, and fun activities that everyone can enjoy. This 7-day itinerary is designed to ensure a perfect balance of relaxation and adventure for both adults and children, while allowing for plenty of opportunities to experience the island's natural and cultural offerings.

Day 1: Arrival and Settling In

Morning: Arrival

- **Arrive in Skiathos** and check into your family-friendly accommodation, such as a beachside hotel or a spacious villa with kitchen facilities.
- Settle in and take some time to rest after your journey.

Afternoon: Skiathos Town Exploration

- **Stroll around Skiathos Town** (Chora). Explore the charming narrow streets, shops, and cafes. Let the children enjoy some ice cream while you pick up some souvenirs.

- Head to **Bourtzi Peninsula Park**, where the kids can run around in the green space and enjoy the view of the port.

Evening: Dinner at a Family-Friendly Taverna

- Have a relaxed dinner at a family-friendly restaurant like **Taverna To Steki**, which offers delicious Greek cuisine in a casual setting. The menu has plenty of child-friendly options like grilled meats, pasta, and fresh salads.

Day 2: Beach Day at Koukounaries and Banana Beach

Morning: Koukounaries Beach

- Start the day at **Koukounaries Beach**, one of the most family-friendly beaches on the island. Its shallow waters, soft sand, and calm environment make it ideal for children to play and swim.
- Rent an umbrella and enjoy the shade while the kids build sandcastles or play in the shallow waters.

Afternoon: Banana Beach

- After lunch, take a short walk or drive to **Banana Beach**. This beach is perfect for a relaxed afternoon. The kids can enjoy playing in the sand or swimming in the calm waters, while adults can relax under the umbrellas.

Evening: Seaside Dinner

- For dinner, head to **Kipos Taverna**, a laid-back family restaurant with a lovely outdoor seating area. The menu includes many options that children will enjoy, such as **moussaka** and **souvlaki**.

Day 3: Boat Trip to Lalaria Beach and Nearby Islands

Morning: Boat Ride to Lalaria Beach

- Begin your day with a **boat trip to Lalaria Beach**, a beautiful and secluded beach with white pebbles and crystal-clear waters. While this beach is more dramatic, it is still an exciting adventure for children to experience the boat ride and explore this unique location.
- Take plenty of snacks, drinks, and sunscreen for a comfortable experience on the boat.

Afternoon: Visit Nearby Islands

- After spending some time at Lalaria, take the boat to nearby islands and hidden coves, where the kids can enjoy exploring the waters, swimming, and snorkelling (many boat tours offer snorkelling gear for children).

Evening: Relax and Unwind

- Head back to Skiathos and have dinner at **Taverna La Scala**, a cozy spot offering a relaxed atmosphere and a variety of Greek and international dishes for all ages.

Day 4: Cultural and Educational Day

Morning: Skiathos Castle and Kastro Village

- Visit **Skiathos Castle** and explore the ancient ruins. The walk to the castle offers fantastic views of the island and is a great educational experience for older children to learn about the island's history.
- Walk through **Kastro Village**, a peaceful, historical site where families can enjoy exploring the old stone houses and taking in the panoramic views.

Afternoon: Museum of Skiathos

- After lunch, take the family to the **Museum of Skiathos**, where children can learn more about the island's culture and history. The museum showcases traditional costumes, religious icons, and artifacts that tell the story of the island's past.

Evening: Dinner with Local Flavor

- Enjoy dinner at **Ouzeri Loukia**, a relaxed spot where the whole family can enjoy small plates like **tzatziki**, **souvlaki**, and **grilled vegetables**. The casual atmosphere makes it ideal for families with children.

Day 5: Fun Day at Skiathos Water Park and Beaches

Morning: Skiathos Water Park

- Start the day with a fun family trip to the **Skiathos Water Park**. The park offers a variety of water slides, wave pools, and play areas for children of all ages, making it the perfect spot for a thrilling and refreshing day out.

Afternoon: Lunch and Beach Fun

- After enjoying the water park, head to **Achladies Beach**, which is just a short drive away. This beach is quieter and ideal for families. The shallow waters make it great for the little ones, and there are plenty of shaded areas for relaxation.

Evening: Family Dinner by the Sea

- Enjoy a beachside dinner at **Kavouras Taverna**, a family-friendly spot known for its fresh seafood and casual atmosphere. The kids will love the relaxed vibe and the variety of menu options, including pasta and grilled meats.

Day 6: Nature and Wildlife Exploration

Morning: Hike in Skiathos Nature Reserve

- Take a morning **hike through the Skiathos Nature Reserve**. The reserve offers easy trails suitable for children, where they can enjoy exploring nature and spotting wildlife, including rabbits, birds, and other small animals. The walk is peaceful and offers beautiful views of the island.

Afternoon: Visit Papadiamantis House

- In the afternoon, take the family to **Papadiamantis House**, which is dedicated to the famous Greek author who lived on the island. The museum is small and interactive, making it suitable for children to learn about Greek literature and history.

Evening: Traditional Dinner

- Have a traditional Greek dinner at **The Garden Taverna**, which offers a welcoming atmosphere for families. Enjoy classic Greek dishes such as **giouvetsi** (Greek stew) and **souvlaki**, with a variety of options for younger guests.

Day 7: Leisure Day and Farewell Dinner

Morning: Beach Fun at Vassilias Beach

- For your last day, spend the morning at **Vassilias Beach**, a peaceful family-friendly spot. It's quieter than other beaches, making it ideal for a relaxing last day. You can rent kayaks, pedal boats, or simply swim and enjoy the calm waters.

Afternoon: Last-Minute Shopping and Exploration

- After the beach, head to Skiathos Town for some **last-minute shopping**. Visit local shops for souvenirs like handmade jewelry, ceramics, and traditional Greek products.

Evening: Farewell Dinner

- For your final dinner, enjoy a relaxed meal at **Skiathos Yacht Club**, which offers a family-friendly environment and excellent Greek cuisine. Celebrate the end of your family getaway with a delicious meal, reflecting on the memorable moments you've shared.

This 7-day itinerary is packed with a mix of relaxation and fun activities that the entire family can enjoy. From beautiful beaches and water parks to cultural sites and nature walks, Skiathos offers a diverse range of experiences for families. Whether you're lounging on the beach, exploring ancient ruins, or enjoying local delicacies, this itinerary ensures a balanced, enjoyable, and stress-free family vacation.

Chapter 9. Sustainable Travel

9.1 Eco-Friendly Activities in Skiathos

Skiathos, known for its natural beauty, is increasingly becoming a destination where sustainable and eco-friendly travel practices are being embraced. Whether you're an environmentally conscious traveler or simply looking to enjoy the island's nature in a responsible way, there are plenty of activities that allow you to explore Skiathos while minimizing your environmental impact. Below are some of the best eco-friendly activities to enjoy on the island.

1. Hiking and Nature Walks

Skiathos offers a wide variety of **hiking trails** that let you explore the island's stunning landscapes in an eco-friendly way. The island's nature reserves and forested areas are home to diverse wildlife and plant species. By walking instead of driving, you can enjoy the natural beauty of the island while reducing your carbon footprint.

- **Skiathos Nature Reserve**: A peaceful haven for birdwatchers and wildlife enthusiasts. The trails here are easy to navigate and provide the opportunity to explore lush forests, olive groves, and Mediterranean flora.
- **Kastro Trail**: A relatively easy hike that takes you through olive groves and offers scenic views of the island and the surrounding sea.
- **Evangelistria Monastery Trail**: This trail leads you to the island's historic monastery, offering the chance to connect with nature and history. Along the way, enjoy the natural surroundings while learning about the island's cultural heritage.

2. Cycling Tours

Cycling is one of the most eco-friendly ways to explore Skiathos. There are several **cycling tours** available on the island, where you can discover hidden spots, remote beaches, and tranquil areas. Several companies offer bike rentals, including electric bikes, which reduce your environmental impact while allowing you to cover more ground with ease.

- **Skiathos Cycling Tours**: These tours take you through scenic routes, forests, and coastal roads, allowing you to enjoy the island's biodiversity. Many tours are guided by locals who provide insight into the region's flora and fauna, making for an educational and eco-friendly experience.

3. Kayaking and Paddleboarding

For a more water-based adventure, kayaking and paddleboarding are wonderful ways to explore the crystal-clear waters of Skiathos while minimizing environmental impact. These activities allow you to enjoy the natural beauty of the coastline at a slow, peaceful pace, avoiding the use of motorized boats.

- **Kayaking in Lalaria Bay**: One of the island's most beautiful beaches, accessible by kayak. Paddle through turquoise waters and explore the stunning rock formations and caves of Lalaria.
- **Paddleboarding at Koukounaries**: This peaceful beach is ideal for paddleboarding, offering calm waters and an opportunity to enjoy the surrounding nature from the sea.

4. Sustainable Boat Tours

While traditional boat tours often involve larger motorized vessels, **eco-friendly boat tours** are increasingly popular in Skiathos. These tours often utilize smaller, more sustainable boats, sometimes even powered by solar energy. They provide a more eco-conscious way to explore the island's stunning coastline and nearby islands.

- **Eco-Friendly Sailing Tours**: Choose a sailing tour where the boat uses wind power rather than a motor, offering a quieter and more sustainable way to see the island from the water.
- **Wildlife Watching Tours**: Join a guided eco-tour that focuses on marine life, such as dolphins, seals, and sea turtles. These tours are designed to be informative and have a low environmental impact.

5. Beach Clean-Up Activities

Several local organizations and environmental groups in Skiathos organize **beach clean-up activities**, where volunteers can help clean the island's beautiful beaches while also learning about the importance of preserving marine environments.

- **Skiathos Environmental Group**: Participate in a community clean-up day or even start your own initiative with friends and family. Removing litter from beaches not only preserves the beauty of the island but also helps protect the local marine life.

6. Visiting Eco-Friendly Accommodation

Several accommodations in Skiathos are adopting **eco-friendly practices**, such as energy-saving systems, waste recycling, and water conservation efforts. Staying in these hotels and resorts ensures that your travel choices align with sustainable practices.

- **Eco Hotels in Skiathos**: Look for hotels that have green certifications or those that are committed to using renewable energy sources, reducing plastic waste, and supporting local food production. These accommodations often also offer educational materials and activities focused on sustainability.

7. Supporting Local, Sustainable Agriculture

Skiathos is home to several **organic farms** and small-scale local producers who focus on sustainable agriculture. Visiting these farms or purchasing local, organic products is a wonderful way to support the island's eco-friendly farming practices and enjoy the freshest produce.

- **Farm Visits**: Take a tour of local organic farms where you can see firsthand how food is grown in an environmentally friendly way. Many farms also offer workshops on organic gardening, making it a great educational experience for children and adults alike.
- **Farmers' Markets**: Skiathos has several farmers' markets where you can purchase locally grown, organic products like fruits, vegetables, herbs, and honey, helping to support the local economy while reducing food miles.

8. Volunteering for Conservation Efforts

For those looking to make a more hands-on impact, **volunteering with local environmental groups** can be a rewarding way to give back to the island. Skiathos has several conservation initiatives aimed at protecting the island's flora, fauna, and marine life.

- **Skiathos Conservation Projects**: Participate in projects focused on protecting the island's biodiversity, such as the conservation of sea turtles or the preservation of natural habitats. Volunteering can give you a deeper understanding of the environmental challenges faced by the island and contribute to its preservation.

Skiathos offers numerous eco-friendly activities that allow visitors to explore the island's natural beauty while minimizing their environmental impact. From hiking and cycling to sustainable boat tours and volunteering opportunities, there are many ways to enjoy the island responsibly. By incorporating these eco-friendly practices into your travel plans, you can help protect the island's fragile ecosystems and contribute to the growing movement of sustainable tourism on Skiathos.

9.2 Sustainable Tourism on Skiathos

As travel and tourism continue to grow, destinations like Skiathos are increasingly focusing on sustainability to ensure that their natural beauty and cultural heritage are preserved for future generations. Sustainable tourism on Skiathos is about finding a balance between the economic benefits of tourism and the protection of the island's environment, culture, and local community. Below is an overview of the initiatives and practices that make Skiathos a leader in sustainable tourism, as well as ways travelers can contribute to these efforts.

1. Green Certifications and Eco-Friendly Accommodations

Skiathos is home to a growing number of **eco-certified accommodations** that implement sustainable practices, such as energy-efficient technologies, water conservation systems, and waste reduction strategies. Many hotels, resorts, and villas on the island are now adopting eco-friendly practices to minimize their environmental footprint.

- **Energy and Water Conservation**: Several accommodations use renewable energy sources such as solar panels and have energy-efficient lighting and appliances to reduce energy consumption. Water-saving devices, like low-flow showers and rainwater collection systems, are also common.
- **Waste Reduction**: Many hotels have implemented recycling programs, reduced plastic waste by offering refillable water stations, and use eco-friendly cleaning products.
- **Green Certifications**: Look for accommodations with certifications from organizations such as the **Green Key** or the **EU Ecolabel**, which demonstrate a commitment to environmental sustainability.

2. Supporting Local and Sustainable Food Systems

Skiathos places great emphasis on promoting **local, organic food**, which supports the island's farmers and reduces the environmental impact associated with food transportation. Many restaurants, tavernas, and cafes now feature locally sourced and organic ingredients on their menus, reducing the carbon footprint of food production.

- **Farm-to-Table Dining**: Many establishments now source fresh produce, fish, and meat from local farmers and fishermen, ensuring that the food is not only fresh but also sustainably produced.

- **Sustainable Seafood**: The island's tavernas focus on sustainable fishing practices, with a growing emphasis on using fish and seafood caught through responsible methods that do not harm the marine ecosystem.
- **Eco-Friendly Markets**: The **local farmers' markets** on Skiathos are a great way to support sustainable agriculture. These markets sell organic produce, honey, herbs, and local artisan products, allowing you to contribute to the local economy while minimizing your environmental impact.

3. Environmental Protection and Marine Conservation

Skiathos is taking significant steps to protect its delicate marine ecosystems, particularly in areas like the **Skiathos Marine Park**, which is dedicated to preserving the biodiversity of the surrounding waters and islands. The park is home to species such as the Mediterranean monk seal, sea turtles, and various marine birds.

- **Marine Conservation Efforts**: The island has implemented various conservation programs to protect its marine life. These include monitoring and safeguarding nesting sites for sea turtles, which nest along the island's beaches, and ensuring sustainable fishing practices.
- **Plastic-Free Initiatives**: Skiathos has been working to reduce plastic waste on the island. Many businesses now encourage the use of reusable items, and some have switched to biodegradable products, such as straws and utensils.
- **Volunteer Programs**: Several organizations, such as the **Skiathos Environmental Group**, organize beach clean-up programs and marine conservation efforts. Tourists can participate in these programs, directly contributing to the preservation of the island's beaches and waters.

4. Eco-Friendly Transportation

Skiathos is increasingly focusing on providing **sustainable transportation options** for visitors. The island encourages low-carbon alternatives to get around, making it easier for travelers to explore while minimizing their environmental impact.

- **Electric Vehicles (EVs)**: Car rental agencies on Skiathos now offer electric vehicles (EVs) for tourists. These eco-friendly cars have zero emissions and are a great way to explore the island without contributing to air pollution.
- **Cycling and Walking**: As part of its commitment to sustainability, Skiathos promotes cycling and walking as modes of transportation. The island offers bike rentals, and there are many scenic walking trails for those who wish to explore the natural beauty of the island in an environmentally friendly way.

- **Public Transportation**: The island's bus network is another sustainable option, offering an affordable and low-emission way to travel between key destinations like the beaches, Skiathos Town, and the airport.

5. Eco-Tourism Experiences and Activities

Eco-tourism has become a key part of Skiathos' tourism offerings, with a variety of activities designed to allow visitors to enjoy the island's natural beauty while minimizing their environmental impact.

- **Eco-Friendly Boat Tours**: Many boat operators now offer eco-friendly tours that use wind-powered or small, non-motorized boats to explore Skiathos' coastline and nearby islands. These tours emphasize the importance of marine conservation and allow guests to witness the island's unique marine life.
- **Wildlife Watching**: Skiathos is a fantastic place for wildlife enthusiasts, with opportunities to see marine life such as dolphins, seals, and various seabirds. Sustainable wildlife watching tours promote conservation awareness and educate visitors on the importance of protecting these species.
- **Hiking and Nature Walks**: Skiathos has numerous hiking trails, such as those around the **Skiathos Nature Reserve**. These trails not only provide an opportunity to connect with nature but also raise awareness about the preservation of the island's flora and fauna.

6. Promoting Local Craft and Sustainable Souvenirs

Supporting local artisans and buying sustainable souvenirs is another important aspect of sustainable tourism on Skiathos. By purchasing locally-made crafts, tourists contribute to the island's economy while reducing the environmental cost associated with mass-produced, imported goods.

- **Handmade Souvenirs**: Look for locally crafted items such as **ceramics**, **woven textiles**, **handmade jewelry**, and **olive oil products**. Many of these goods are made with traditional techniques that have minimal environmental impact.
- **Sustainable Products**: Shops and boutiques in Skiathos are increasingly offering eco-friendly souvenirs, such as products made from recycled materials, biodegradable items, and items created with fair-trade practices.

7. Community Involvement and Responsible Tourism

Skiathos is committed to fostering a sense of community involvement in tourism, ensuring that local residents benefit from the island's growing popularity. The island's tourism sector works closely with local businesses, artisans, and community groups to ensure that economic benefits are shared equitably and that tourism is managed in a way that preserves the island's heritage and culture.

- **Support for Local Businesses**: Many of the island's businesses, from family-owned tavernas to local shops, rely on tourism for their livelihood. Choosing to dine at local restaurants, buy souvenirs from local artisans, and stay at locally-owned accommodations helps keep the island's economy thriving.
- **Cultural Respect**: Sustainable tourism in Skiathos also involves respecting the local culture and traditions. Visitors are encouraged to embrace the island's lifestyle, participate in local festivals, and learn about its history and heritage.

Sustainable tourism is at the heart of Skiathos' approach to welcoming visitors, and the island is dedicated to ensuring that its natural beauty, cultural heritage, and local community are preserved for future generations. By staying at eco-friendly accommodations, supporting local businesses, and choosing sustainable activities, visitors can help contribute to the island's sustainability efforts. Whether you're hiking in the nature reserves, participating in conservation programs, or enjoying organic local cuisine, there are many ways to enjoy Skiathos responsibly and sustainably.

9.3 Supporting Local Communities and Businesses in Skiathos

One of the most important aspects of sustainable tourism is ensuring that the economic benefits of tourism are shared with the local communities and businesses that make the destination special. In Skiathos, supporting local communities and businesses is vital to maintaining the island's authentic charm and helping to preserve its cultural heritage. Below are some of the key ways travelers can contribute to the local economy and make a positive impact on the island's residents.

1. Stay in Locally-Owned Accommodations

One of the easiest ways to support the local community while visiting Skiathos is by staying in **locally-owned hotels, guesthouses, and boutique accommodations**. Unlike large international hotel chains, locally owned accommodations are more likely to reinvest profits into the local economy, support local workers, and offer a more authentic, personalized experience.

- **Family-Owned Guesthouses**: Opt for family-run guesthouses or B&Bs, which offer a more intimate stay and often provide the opportunity to interact with locals. Many of these establishments are located in picturesque areas, offering a more authentic experience of Skiathos.
- **Boutique Hotels**: Boutique hotels often focus on sustainability and local charm, offering rooms decorated with locally sourced materials and supporting community-based tourism initiatives.

By choosing these options, you contribute to maintaining the island's heritage and ensuring that the benefits of tourism reach those who are directly invested in preserving its culture.

2. Support Local Restaurants and Taverns

Skiathos boasts a wealth of **traditional Greek restaurants** and **tavernas** that offer delicious, locally sourced meals. Many of these establishments use fresh ingredients from the island's farms and fishermen, giving you the chance to experience authentic Greek cuisine while supporting the local economy.

- **Local Specialties**: Many tavernas offer dishes that feature **locally caught seafood**, **seasonal vegetables**, and **regional meats**. By dining at these establishments, you are helping to promote sustainable farming and fishing practices, ensuring that locals can continue to make a living from their natural resources.
- **Farm-to-Table Dining**: Look for restaurants that source their ingredients from local farmers and food producers. These businesses typically support sustainable agricultural practices and focus on using organic, pesticide-free products.

Supporting these eateries not only helps the local economy but also provides you with a more genuine taste of the island's culture.

3. Buy Locally Made Products and Souvenirs

Skiathos is home to many **artisans and craftspeople** who create beautiful, handmade items that reflect the island's rich cultural traditions. By purchasing locally made products and souvenirs, you help to sustain the island's traditional crafts while also supporting small businesses.

- **Local Art and Handicrafts**: Shops in Skiathos Town and surrounding villages sell items such as **handwoven textiles**, **ceramics**, **wooden crafts**, **olive oil products**, and **jewelry**. These items are often created using traditional techniques passed down through generations, and purchasing them ensures the continuation of these skills.

- **Organic Products**: Many shops on the island offer **organic honey**, **olive oil**, **herbs**. These goods support sustainable agriculture and provide a way for farmers to earn a fair income.
- **Supporting Fair Trade**: Look for stores that specialize in **fair trade** items, which ensure that local artisans and farmers are paid a fair wage for their work. Fair trade practices also focus on environmental sustainability, reducing waste, and promoting ethical production methods.

By purchasing these handmade products, you're contributing directly to the livelihood of local artists, farmers, and producers.

4. Participate in Local Tours and Activities

A great way to immerse yourself in the local culture while supporting small businesses is by booking tours and activities that are operated by local guides and companies. These tours often focus on showcasing the island's unique history, culture, and natural beauty, providing an authentic experience that benefits the local community.

- **Walking Tours**: Join a guided walking tour of **Skiathos Town** or **Kastro**, where local guides share their knowledge of the island's history and culture. These tours provide a personal and enriching experience, and the money you spend goes directly to local guides.
- **Boat Tours**: Book a boat tour with local operators who use smaller, family-run vessels. These eco-friendly tours provide an opportunity to explore Skiathos' coastline, nearby islands, and secluded beaches, while supporting local boat owners and captains.
- **Cultural Experiences**: Participate in workshops that teach local crafts, cooking classes, or olive oil tours. These activities are often led by locals and provide you with a chance to learn more about traditional practices while supporting local artisans and businesses.

By choosing locally operated tours and experiences, you help to sustain the island's tourism industry and support those who are working to preserve its culture and heritage.

5. Visit Local Markets and Farmers' Markets

The island's **farmers' markets** are an excellent place to purchase fresh, organic produce and products directly from local growers and producers. These markets help maintain traditional agricultural practices while allowing visitors to sample some of the island's freshest and most authentic foods.

- **Skiathos Farmers' Market**: Located in Skiathos Town, this market is filled with fresh fruits, vegetables, local cheeses, and homemade jams. It's a great way to support local farmers and enjoy the best of the island's produce.
- **Seasonal Produce**: Depending on when you visit, you can find different local products such as strawberries, olives, figs, and fresh herbs, all grown on the island. Purchasing directly from farmers ensures that they receive a fair price for their goods.
- **Local Specialty Products**: In addition to fresh produce, the markets also sell products like **local honey**, **handmade soaps**, **herbal teas**, and **sweets**. These items make for perfect souvenirs while supporting sustainable practices.

Shopping at local markets allows you to directly support the island's agricultural sector, ensuring that traditional farming techniques continue to thrive.

6. Respect Local Traditions and Culture

A key element of sustainable tourism is **cultural respect**. Visitors are encouraged to learn about and respect the traditions and customs of Skiathos, ensuring that tourism does not disrupt the local way of life.

- **Participate in Festivals**: Skiathos hosts several traditional festivals throughout the year, including religious celebrations and local cultural events. By attending these festivals, you not only enjoy an authentic experience but also support local performers, artisans, and food vendors.
- **Learn the Local Language**: While most people on the island speak English, learning a few basic Greek phrases can go a long way in showing respect for the local culture. It also creates stronger bonds with locals and enhances your travel experience.
- **Support Local Initiatives**: Look for businesses and initiatives that focus on preserving the island's culture, such as museums, craft workshops, and historical sites. These establishments often rely on tourism to maintain and share the island's rich heritage.

By respecting local customs and traditions, you help preserve the island's cultural identity while ensuring that tourism contributes positively to the community.

Supporting local communities and businesses is a cornerstone of sustainable tourism in Skiathos. From choosing locally-owned accommodations and dining at family-run tavernas to purchasing handmade crafts and participating in cultural experiences, there are countless ways for travelers to make a positive impact. By spending your money thoughtfully and engaging with the island's community, you contribute to the long-term sustainability of Skiathos and ensure that it remains a vibrant, thriving destination for years to come.

Chapter 10. Seasonal Events and Festivals

10.1 Summer Festivals (Music, Art, and Culture)

Skiathos is known for its lively and vibrant **summer festival scene**, where a range of music, art, and cultural events take place throughout the warm months. These festivals highlight the island's rich heritage, local talent, and its strong connection to the arts. Whether you're a fan of traditional Greek music, contemporary performances, or classical art exhibitions, there's something to experience for everyone during the summer season. Here are some of the most notable events that you can enjoy in Skiathos during the summer.

1. Skiathos Chamber Music Festival

- **Location**: Skiathos Town, various venues
- **Time**: July – August
- **Price**: Varies (Tickets typically range from €10 to €50 depending on the performance)
- **Website**: Skiathos Chamber Music Festival (if available)
- **Opening Hours**: Performances typically start in the evening, around 7:00 PM – 9:00 PM

Description: The Skiathos Chamber Music Festival is a prestigious event that attracts classical music lovers from all over the world. Held in various venues across the island, including historical buildings and intimate settings, this festival features talented musicians performing a wide range of chamber music, from classical to contemporary pieces. The festival aims to provide high-quality music in an intimate setting, and it often features performances by internationally renowned artists.

- **Key Features**: Classical chamber music performances, international artists, intimate venues, high-quality acoustics.
- **Visitor Services**: Guided tours of the venues, tickets available online or at local box offices, accessible seating for those with mobility needs.

Why Visit: If you're a lover of classical music and enjoy discovering hidden gems in historical settings, this festival is the perfect experience. The intimate venues and world-class musicians create a magical atmosphere that enhances the charm of Skiathos.

2. Skiathos International Film Festival

- **Location**: Skiathos Town, various open-air theaters
- **Time**: June – July
- **Price**: Varies (Tickets typically range from €5 to €15)
- **Website**: Skiathos International Film Festival (if available)
- **Opening Hours**: Screenings generally start at 8:00 PM – 10:00 PM

Description: The Skiathos International Film Festival is a celebrated cultural event that attracts film enthusiasts and filmmakers from around the world. It features a range of independent films, from documentaries to feature-length productions, with a focus on emerging filmmakers and diverse storytelling. The festival's unique setting, often held in open-air theaters overlooking the Aegean Sea, offers a perfect blend of cinema and nature.

- **Key Features**: Independent films, international filmmakers, open-air screenings, diverse genres including documentaries, features, and shorts.
- **Visitor Services**: Tickets available at the festival venue or online, guided tours for those interested in the history of Greek cinema.

Why Visit: The Skiathos International Film Festival offers an exceptional cultural experience for cinephiles, and the island's stunning open-air theaters provide a beautiful backdrop for a night at the movies. It's an opportunity to discover new films and support emerging talent in the film industry.

3. Skiathos Music and Dance Festival

- **Location**: Skiathos Town, main squares and open-air venues
- **Time**: June – September
- **Price**: Free entry to many events, some ticketed performances (€5 to €30)
- **Website**: Skiathos Music and Dance Festival (if available)
- **Opening Hours**: Performances generally take place throughout the evening, from 7:00 PM to midnight

Description: The Skiathos Music and Dance Festival celebrates the rich cultural traditions of Greece, with a special focus on local music and dance forms. Visitors can enjoy performances of traditional Greek music, folk dances, and theatrical presentations in outdoor venues that showcase the island's lively atmosphere. The festival often features local musicians, as well as performers from across Greece, and is a great way to experience the authentic spirit of Skiathos.

- **Key Features**: Greek folk music, traditional dance performances, local musicians, open-air venues.
- **Visitor Services**: Free and ticketed events, guided tours explaining the history of Greek music and dance, event schedules available at local tourist offices.

Why Visit: If you are keen to immerse yourself in Greek culture, this festival offers a fantastic opportunity to experience traditional Greek music and dance in a vibrant, celebratory environment. It's a family-friendly event with something for everyone to enjoy.

4. Skiathos Arts Festival

- **Location**: Various venues in Skiathos Town and surrounding areas
- **Time**: July – August
- **Price**: Varies by event (typically €5 to €20)
- **Website**: Skiathos Arts Festival (if available)
- **Opening Hours**: Events often run in the evening, from 6:00 PM – 10:00 PM

Description: The Skiathos Arts Festival is a multidisciplinary event that features a variety of performances and exhibitions in the fields of music, theater, visual arts, and literature. The festival provides a platform for both Greek and international artists to showcase their work and engage with the local community. Visitors can enjoy a range of performances, from contemporary theater productions to art exhibitions, live readings, and interactive workshops.

- **Key Features**: Visual arts exhibitions, theater performances, literary readings, multi-disciplinary performances, international and local artists.
- **Visitor Services**: Event schedules available in advance, tickets available online or at local offices, guided tours of exhibitions and performances.

Why Visit: The Skiathos Arts Festival is perfect for those seeking a diverse cultural experience, with the opportunity to explore various art forms in an intimate and welcoming environment. It also gives visitors the chance to interact with artists and learn about different creative processes.

5. Skiathos Classical Music Festival

- **Location**: Various venues in Skiathos Town
- **Time**: July – August
- **Price**: Varies (Typically €10 to €30 depending on performance)
- **Website**: Skiathos Classical Music Festival (if available)
- **Opening Hours**: Performances usually begin at 7:00 PM

Description: This festival is a highlight for classical music enthusiasts, bringing together world-class musicians for a series of performances that take place in some of Skiathos' most scenic and acoustically rich locations. The festival offers a chance to experience both well-known classical works as well as lesser-known pieces performed by distinguished artists.

- **Key Features**: Classical music performances, renowned international musicians, unique venues with excellent acoustics.
- **Visitor Services**: Event programs available on-site, tickets sold at local outlets and online, accessible venues for all visitors.

Why Visit: For lovers of classical music, this festival provides an unparalleled opportunity to enjoy world-class performances in one of the most beautiful settings in the Mediterranean.

Skiathos' summer festivals offer something for every visitor, whether you're a music lover, an art enthusiast, or someone interested in learning more about Greek culture. The variety of events—ranging from classical music and theater to folk dancing and visual arts—ensures that no matter when you visit, you'll have the chance to enjoy something unique and memorable. These festivals not only provide entertainment but also contribute to the local community and economy, making them a great way to support the island's cultural landscape.

10.2 Religious Festivals (Holy Week, Feast Days)

Skiathos is a deeply religious island, and its **religious festivals** are an important part of its cultural fabric. These celebrations, marked by centuries-old traditions, offer visitors a unique opportunity to experience the island's spiritual life, with beautiful rituals, processions, and feasts. Whether you're a spiritual traveler or simply interested in experiencing the local culture, these religious festivals provide an intimate and authentic glimpse into Greek Orthodox practices. Here are some of the most significant religious festivals on Skiathos:

1. Holy Week (Pascha)

- **Location**: Throughout the island, with a focus on Skiathos Town and surrounding villages
- **Time**: Easter, usually in April (dates vary based on the Orthodox Christian calendar)
- **Price**: Free to attend, but donations for religious purposes are often accepted
- **Website**: No official website (local church announcements available)

- **Opening Hours**: Services begin on Palm Sunday and culminate with midnight Easter service

Description: Holy Week, or **Pascha**, is the most important religious festival on the Greek Orthodox calendar, and it is celebrated with great fervor across Skiathos. The week-long celebration begins with Palm Sunday and includes processions, special church services, and cultural events leading up to **Holy Saturday**, when a midnight mass is held to mark the resurrection of Christ. The entire island is involved in the celebrations, with many locals attending church services every evening.

On **Holy Saturday night**, the resurrection service is a significant event, with a procession starting at the main church in Skiathos Town, followed by the lighting of candles as the faithful walk through the streets, symbolizing the victory of light over darkness. The festive meal that follows, with lamb and other local dishes, marks the end of the fasting period.

- **Key Features**: Midnight mass, candlelit processions, traditional Easter feasts, church services throughout the week.
- **Visitor Services**: Guided tours explaining the significance of each service, candle rentals for the procession, local restaurants serving traditional Easter dishes post-service.

Why Visit: Holy Week on Skiathos is a profound experience for anyone interested in Greek Orthodox religious customs. The island's spiritual devotion is palpable, and the processions and ceremonies are truly awe-inspiring. It's a time of community bonding, reflection, and celebration, making it a meaningful time to experience the island's culture.

2. Feast of the Assumption of the Virgin Mary (15th August)

- **Location**: Various churches on Skiathos, especially the **Church of the Virgin Mary of Kounistra** and **Church of Panagia Evangelistria**
- **Time**: 15th August
- **Price**: Free to attend, donations accepted
- **Website**: No official website (local church information available)
- **Opening Hours**: Services throughout the day, with a large procession in the evening

Description: The **Feast of the Assumption of the Virgin Mary** is another major religious celebration on Skiathos, observed on the 15th of August. It commemorates the assumption of the Virgin Mary into heaven and is celebrated with various church services, processions, and cultural events. The most significant of these takes place in the **Church of Panagia Evangelistria**, one of the island's holiest sites, where pilgrims gather from all over the region to take part in the religious ceremonies.

In addition to the religious observances, this feast day is celebrated with traditional Greek music, dancing, and feasting, often lasting well into the night. Locals prepare an array of delicious dishes, including lamb, pilaf, and sweets, and share them with family and friends.

- **Key Features**: Church services, evening procession, local feasts, music, and dancing.
- **Visitor Services**: Visitors are encouraged to join the processions and take part in the celebrations, although some local customs may require respect for religious traditions. Local eateries offer special holiday menus.

Why Visit: This feast day is an extraordinary way to witness the reverence the locals have for the Virgin Mary, as well as to partake in the joyful, community-centered celebration that combines religion, culture, and hospitality. It's a must-see for visitors who want to experience the island's spiritual and festive atmosphere.

3. Feast of St. Nicholas (6th December)

- **Location**: Church of St. Nicholas in Skiathos Town, and other churches dedicated to St. Nicholas
- **Time**: 6th December
- **Price**: Free to attend
- **Website**: No official website (local church announcements available)
- **Opening Hours**: Church services throughout the day, starting early in the morning

Description: The **Feast of St. Nicholas** is another important religious celebration on Skiathos, honoring the patron saint of sailors. The island's close connection to the sea makes this feast particularly significant, and it's a time when locals gather in the **Church of St. Nicholas** in Skiathos Town and in other smaller chapels across the island to offer prayers for protection and guidance on the seas.

This celebration includes a religious service in the morning and often culminates in a procession to the church in the evening. Sailors and those who work at sea are especially involved in the celebrations, and many boats are decorated with flowers and offerings. St. Nicholas is considered the protector of sailors, and his feast day is an important occasion for those who depend on the sea for their livelihood.

- **Key Features**: Church services, sea-related blessings, processions, boat decorations.

- **Visitor Services**: Visitors can observe the service and join the procession. Local shops may close during the service hours, but restaurants typically remain open, offering traditional seafood dishes.

Why Visit: The Feast of St. Nicholas is an interesting event for those with an interest in maritime traditions and the cultural significance of the sea to Skiathos. Visitors will find the celebrations to be meaningful and deeply rooted in the island's history and community spirit.

4. Feast of St. George (23rd April)

- **Location**: Churches dedicated to St. George, such as the **Church of St. George in Koukounaries**
- **Time**: 23rd April
- **Price**: Free to attend
- **Website**: No official website (local church announcements available)
- **Opening Hours**: Church services throughout the day

Description: The **Feast of St. George** is celebrated on the 23rd of April and is another important religious event for the island's community. St. George is considered a protector against evil, and his feast day is marked by church services, prayers, and community gatherings. The most significant observance takes place at the **Church of St. George in Koukounaries**, but other smaller chapels on the island also hold services in his honor.

The festival is more low-key compared to other feast days but is still an important occasion for the local community, particularly those with ties to the farming and rural traditions of the island.

- **Key Features**: Church services, traditional feasts, local processions.
- **Visitor Services**: Visitors are welcome to attend the services and join in the local celebrations, which often include home-cooked meals and traditional Greek dishes.

Why Visit: The Feast of St. George offers a quieter but still deeply meaningful experience of the island's religious life. It's a great event for those seeking a more relaxed atmosphere while still being able to witness the island's devotion and cultural practices.

Religious festivals on Skiathos are a wonderful way to experience the island's deep-rooted spiritual and cultural traditions. From the grandeur of **Holy Week** to the more intimate celebrations of **St. George's Feast**, these events provide visitors with a chance to immerse themselves in local customs, witness beautiful ceremonies, and engage with the island's warm and welcoming community. Whether you're visiting for the **Feast of the Assumption** or the **Feast of St. Nicholas**, each festival offers a unique insight into the island's religious and cultural life.

10.3 Off-Season Activities and Events

While Skiathos is best known for its summer tourist rush, the off-season months (autumn, winter, and early spring) also offer a wealth of experiences for visitors who prefer a quieter, more relaxed atmosphere. During this time, the island is less crowded, and you can enjoy the beauty of its natural landscapes, historical sites, and local culture without the typical hustle and bustle. Whether you're looking for a peaceful retreat, outdoor adventures, or cultural events, Skiathos in the off-season has much to offer. Here's a look at some of the top off-season activities and events to consider:

1. Hiking and Nature Walks

- **Location**: Throughout the island, with popular trails in **Koukounaries**, **Mandraki**, and the **Skiathos Nature Reserve**.
- **Time**: Available year-round, best during mild months (October to early May)
- **Price**: Free (Some guided tours may have a fee)
- **Website**: No specific website, local tour operators provide details
- **Opening Hours**: Trails are open throughout the day, from sunrise to sunset

Description: Skiathos' lush landscapes and varied terrain make it a haven for hiking enthusiasts. The off-season is the perfect time to explore the island's hiking trails, as the cooler weather makes the walks more comfortable, and the crowds are thinner. Popular trails include the path to the **Koukounaries Beach** (passing through pine forests), the **Skiathos Nature Reserve**, and the climb to the **Monastery of Panagia Kounistra**.

In the winter and spring months, the island's flora is in full bloom, providing beautiful scenery along the routes. These hikes offer breathtaking views of the island's coastlines, mountains, and hidden gems that are often missed during the busy summer season.

- **Key Features**: Stunning landscapes, tranquil environment, diverse flora and fauna.
- **Visitor Services**: Guided hikes and walking tours are available. Check with local agencies for more details.

Why Visit: Hiking during the off-season allows you to connect with the natural beauty of Skiathos, offering solitude and an opportunity for reflection in some of the island's most pristine areas.

2.Skiathos International Film Festival

- **Location**: **Skiathos Town** and local cinemas
- **Time**: Held annually in late **October** (dates vary)
- **Price**: Around €10-€15 for a film screening
- **Website**: Skiathos Film Festival
- **Opening Hours**: Typically evening screenings from 7:00 PM onwards

Description: The **Skiathos International Film Festival** is an exciting event for movie buffs. Held annually in late October, this festival showcases a range of local and international films, including independent and documentary films. It's a unique opportunity to experience the creative side of Skiathos through the lens of cinema. The event typically features screenings at local theaters and outdoor venues, often accompanied by Q&A sessions with filmmakers.

The off-season atmosphere makes the festival even more special, as it brings together locals and visitors in a relaxed yet vibrant environment, where you can engage with the art of film in a personal way.

- **Key Features**: Independent films, filmmaker Q&As, community engagement.
- **Visitor Services**: Tickets can be purchased at the venue or online, and some screenings include English subtitles.

Why Visit: If you're a film enthusiast, the Skiathos International Film Festival offers a rare chance to enjoy thought-provoking films while also discovering a less touristy side of the island.

3. Local Craft Fairs and Artisan Markets

- **Location**: **Skiathos Town** and other villages (e.g., **Skiathos Old Port**, **Skiathos Town Square**)
- **Time**: Available year-round, with major events during the off-season (late autumn and winter)
- **Price**: Free to enter; items for sale vary in price
- **Website**: No official website (local tourism office provides details)
- **Opening Hours**: Usually open from 10:00 AM to 6:00 PM on weekends and select weekdays

Description: Off-season months on Skiathos offer a great opportunity to explore local craft fairs and artisan markets. During these events, you'll find handmade goods, including jewelry, ceramics, textiles, and artwork, all created by local artisans. These markets are typically held in the more peaceful months, giving visitors a chance to chat with the creators and take home unique souvenirs that support the island's small businesses.

In addition to the markets, some local artists and craftspeople open their workshops to visitors, offering demonstrations of their craft. If you enjoy discovering handmade, one-of-a-kind items, these markets provide a treasure trove of authentic Skiathos products.

- **Key Features**: Handmade jewelry, ceramics, textiles, and artwork.
- **Visitor Services**: Craft demonstrations, personal interactions with artisans, and the option to purchase unique items.

Why Visit: The off-season markets are a hidden gem for those looking to take home meaningful, locally made souvenirs while supporting small businesses on the island.

4. Winter Celebrations and Local Traditions

- **Location**: Throughout Skiathos Town and villages
- **Time**: Late December to early January (Christmas and New Year celebrations), and throughout the off-season
- **Price**: Free, though some events may include optional purchases (e.g., food, crafts)
- **Website**: Local tourism office provides event details
- **Opening Hours**: Various; check local listings for events

Description: While Skiathos isn't known for its winter tourism, the island still hosts a series of intimate, community-centered celebrations during the holiday season. **Christmas** and **New Year's Eve** bring locals together for festive dinners, music, and dancing, with much of the activity centered around Skiathos Town. Visitors can experience local traditions such as the decoration of homes, street performances, and church services.

Additionally, Skiathos celebrates its **Saint Basil's Day** on January 1st with special events. This is the time when locals exchange small gifts and cakes, and the atmosphere is one of warmth and togetherness. The off-season's quieter pace means you can enjoy these cultural experiences at a slower, more relaxed tempo.

- **Key Features**: Holiday feasts, community gatherings, traditional music and dance.
- **Visitor Services**: Special New Year's events, holiday-themed tours, and cultural performances.

Why Visit: For those who appreciate a quieter, more reflective holiday experience, Skiathos' off-season offers a serene escape with a touch of local holiday charm.

Skiathos in the off-season may be less bustling, but it offers a unique array of activities and events that showcase the island's culture, natural beauty, and local traditions. From peaceful nature hikes to unique cultural events like the Skiathos International Film Festival and off-season artisan markets, there's plenty to enjoy during the quieter months. Whether you're looking to unwind in nature, immerse yourself in local life, or attend cultural events, the off-season in Skiathos provides a fresh perspective on the island's offerings.

Chapter 11. Insider Tips and Local Secrets

11.1 Hidden Gems and Secret Spots

Skiathos, while known for its lively beaches and bustling town, holds a wealth of hidden gems and secret spots that many visitors overlook. These secluded locations offer a more authentic and peaceful experience, allowing you to discover the island's lesser-known beauty. Whether you're looking for quiet beaches, hidden caves, or off-the-beaten-path viewpoints, Skiathos has plenty of hidden treasures waiting to be explored.

1. Lalaria Beach

- **Location**: Accessible only by boat from Skiathos Town or other beaches like Koukounaries.
- **Price**: Free
- **Website**: No official website
- **Opening Hours**: Accessible year-round; best visited during the day for the clear blue waters
- **Key Features**: White pebbles, turquoise water, dramatic cliffs

Description:

Lalaria Beach is one of Skiathos' most stunning and secret beaches, famous for its smooth white pebbles and crystal-clear waters. While not easy to reach (you must take a boat), the trip is worth it for its untouched beauty. Surrounded by steep cliffs and rocky outcrops, the beach offers a truly isolated retreat.

Because of its seclusion, Lalaria is perfect for those seeking a quiet escape, away from the larger tourist spots. It is a peaceful haven, ideal for swimming and sunbathing in a serene atmosphere.

- **Visitor Services**: No services are available on the beach itself, so make sure to bring essentials like water, snacks, and sunscreen. Boat tours to the beach typically offer a relaxing journey.

Why Visit: Lalaria is a must-see for nature lovers and those seeking tranquility away from the more tourist-heavy beaches on the island.

2. Skiathos Old Port

- **Location**: Skiathos Town
- **Price**: Free
- **Website**: No official website

- **Opening Hours**: Open year-round
- **Key Features**: Traditional Greek fishing port, local tavernas, scenic views

Description:

While many visitors are drawn to the modern Skiathos Town port, the **Old Port** remains a hidden gem. Nestled away from the more crowded areas, this small harbor is home to traditional wooden fishing boats, quaint tavernas, and charming waterfront cafés. It's the perfect place for a leisurely walk, away from the bustle of the larger port area.

Enjoy the peaceful atmosphere as you sip a coffee or fresh fruit juice while watching the local fishermen go about their daily routines. The Old Port is also an excellent spot for photography, offering picturesque views of the surrounding hills and calm waters.

- **Visitor Services**: Several small cafés and restaurants offer traditional Greek food and drinks, often with no menu—just fresh, locally prepared dishes of the day.

Why Visit: The Old Port gives you a true sense of local life and is the perfect place to relax while soaking up authentic Greek island vibes.

3. The Cave of Papadiamantis

- **Location**: Near Skiathos Town, close to the Papadiamantis House Museum
- **Price**: Free (if accessed from the street)
- **Website**: No official website
- **Opening Hours**: Accessible year-round
- **Key Features**: Historical significance, serene ambiance

Description:

This small but historically significant cave is located just outside Skiathos Town, offering a quiet escape from the town's lively atmosphere. The cave is famous for being the place where the famous Greek author **Alexandros Papadiamantis** once sought refuge and inspiration for his literary works. Surrounded by lush vegetation, the cave provides a peaceful retreat where you can relax, read, or simply enjoy nature.

Though small, it's a great spot for anyone interested in Greek literature and history, providing a direct link to one of the island's most celebrated figures.

- **Visitor Services**: There are no services or guided tours at the cave itself, but you can visit the nearby **Papadiamantis House Museum**, which gives insight into the author's life.

Why Visit: A hidden historical spot that's ideal for quiet reflection and a deeper connection with Skiathos' cultural heritage.

4. Kechria Beach

- **Location**: North of Skiathos Town
- **Price**: Free
- **Website**: No official website
- **Opening Hours**: Open year-round
- **Key Features**: Secluded, rocky coastline, crystal-clear waters, fewer tourists

Description:

Kechria Beach is one of the least crowded beaches on Skiathos, offering a tranquil and more authentic beach experience. The beach is somewhat isolated, with limited access by a bumpy dirt road, making it one of the island's best-kept secrets. The beach is rocky, with crystal-clear water ideal for snorkeling, and it's surrounded by lush vegetation and steep cliffs, adding to its secluded charm.

While it doesn't offer many tourist amenities, the beach's solitude makes it a perfect spot for those who enjoy peace and nature without the crowds.

- **Visitor Services**: No services available on the beach. Visitors should bring their own supplies and snacks.

Why Visit: Kechria Beach is the perfect spot for those seeking solitude, snorkeling, or simply a quiet, unspoiled place to enjoy the sea.

5. The Monastery of Panagia Kounistra

- **Location**: Atop a hill near Skiathos Town
- **Price**: Free
- **Website**: No official website
- **Opening Hours**: Open daily, typically 8:00 AM - 2:00 PM
- **Key Features**: Historical site, beautiful views, religious significance

Description:

The Monastery of **Panagia Kounistra** is one of the most serene and spiritually significant sites on Skiathos. Perched on a hill just outside Skiathos Town, the monastery is dedicated to the Virgin Mary. The monastery is peaceful, offering sweeping views of the island and the Aegean Sea.

Visitors can explore the beautiful white-washed church, wander around the monastery grounds, and enjoy the solitude of this quiet, spiritual retreat. It is a popular spot for locals, but still a hidden gem for many tourists.

- **Visitor Services**: The monastery often welcomes visitors for peaceful reflection, and donations are encouraged to maintain the site. There is no formal visitor center or guided tours, but the surrounding views make the visit worthwhile.

Why Visit: For a peaceful and reflective experience, the Monastery of Panagia Kounistra provides spiritual solace and breathtaking views.

6. The Secret Path to Skiathos' Highest Point

- **Location**: Behind **Skiathos Town**
- **Price**: Free
- **Website**: No official website
- **Opening Hours**: Open year-round, best during daylight hours
- **Key Features**: Panoramic views, peaceful ambiance, off-the-beaten-path trail

Description:
For the more adventurous traveler, the hidden path to Skiathos' highest point is a thrilling experience. This little-known trail winds its way up the hills behind Skiathos Town, offering panoramic views of the entire island and beyond. The path is quite rugged and not well-marked, making it a perfect escape for those seeking solitude and adventure.

Along the way, you'll encounter stunning vistas, serene nature, and perhaps even the occasional local goat. The summit offers a fantastic view of the Aegean Sea and the surrounding islands, making it a great spot for photography or simply enjoying the peace and quiet.

- **Visitor Services**: No services available, it's recommended to bring water, wear sturdy shoes, and take a map.

Why Visit: For a more challenging yet rewarding experience, this hidden trail offers stunning views and the satisfaction of reaching the highest point on the island.

Skiathos is not just about its popular beaches and towns; the island holds a wealth of hidden gems waiting to be discovered by curious and adventurous travelers. From secluded beaches like **Lalaria** to quiet, culturally rich spots like the **Monastery of Panagia Kounistra**, there are many secret places that offer an authentic and peaceful experience far from the crowds. Whether you're hiking to Skiathos' highest peak, exploring historical sites, or simply relaxing on a remote beach, these hidden treasures will make your visit to Skiathos even more special.

11.2 Local Recommendations (Best Views, Underrated Locations)

Skiathos, while famous for its picturesque beaches and lively town, is also home to a number of underrated and lesser-known locations that provide breathtaking views and authentic experiences. These local recommendations are perfect for travelers who want to go beyond the typical tourist spots and discover the island's hidden beauty. Whether it's a secluded viewpoint, a quiet beach, or a charming village, these locations will give you a more intimate and serene view of Skiathos.

1. The View from The Skiathos Bunker

- **Location**: Near Skiathos Town, off the road to **Koukounaries Beach**
- **Price**: Free
- **Website**: No official website
- **Opening Hours**: Open year-round, best during daylight hours
- **Key Features**: Panoramic views, historical site

Description:

One of the island's best-kept secrets, the **Skiathos Bunker** offers stunning panoramic views of Skiathos Town and its surrounding islands. Situated on a hill, the old military bunker is an underrated viewpoint that provides one of the best sights on the island. The dramatic view over the blue waters of the Aegean Sea, with the backdrop of Skiathos' lush green hills, is truly spectacular, especially during sunset when the colors of the sky reflect in the sea.

- **Why Visit**: Perfect for photography or simply enjoying a quiet moment with an unparalleled view of the Island.

2. Vromolimnos Beach

- **Location**: South of Skiathos Town, near **Koukounaries**
- **Price**: Free
- **Website**: No official website
- **Opening Hours**: Open year-round
- **Key Features**: Quiet beach, clear waters, family-friendly

Description:

While **Koukounaries Beach** is often busy with tourists, **Vromolimnos Beach**, a nearby hidden gem, offers a quieter and more laid-back alternative. Surrounded by lush pine trees and crystal-clear water, this secluded beach is perfect for those who enjoy a peaceful atmosphere. The water is shallow, making it ideal for families with young children or those who prefer a more relaxing swimming experience.

- **Why Visit**: This beach is a perfect escape from the crowds, offering serenity and beauty without the hustle and bustle of more popular spots.

3. The Panagia Evangelistria Monastery

- **Location**: Just outside **Skiathos Town**
- **Price**: Free
- **Website**: No official website
- **Opening Hours**: Open daily, typically 8:00 AM - 3:00 PM
- **Key Features**: Historical site, beautiful views, peaceful atmosphere

Description:

 The **Monastery of Panagia Evangelistria** is an important religious and historical site on Skiathos. Nestled in the hills, this peaceful monastery offers stunning views of the surrounding countryside and the sea. The interior of the monastery is beautifully decorated, with intricate icons and religious artifacts. While not as well-known as other sites, it holds a special place in the hearts of locals. The monastery is often less crowded, giving visitors a serene and contemplative experience.

- **Why Visit**: Visit for its spiritual atmosphere and scenic views that encompass the beauty of the island, away from the typical tourist crowds.

4. Skiathos Windmill

- **Location**: Near **Skiathos Town**, on a small hill overlooking the town
- **Price**: Free
- **Website**: No official website
- **Opening Hours**: Open year-round
- **Key Features**: Iconic landmark, great for photos, panoramic views

Description:

 The **Skiathos Windmill** is an iconic feature of the island's skyline, offering one of the best views of **Skiathos Town** and its surroundings. This traditional windmill stands atop a hill and is often overlooked by visitors. From here, you can enjoy sweeping views of the town, the port, and the Aegean Sea beyond. It's a fantastic spot for photography, especially at sunrise or sunset when the light bathes the island in warm, golden hues.

- **Why Visit**: A great vantage point to appreciate the beauty of Skiathos from a different angle, with fewer crowds compared to other view locations.

5. Troulos Beach

- **Location**: South of Skiathos Town, near **Koukounaries**
- **Price**: Free
- **Website**: No official website
- **Opening Hours**: Open year-round
- **Key Features**: Shallow waters, less crowded, family-friendly

Description:

Troulos Beach, located to the south of Skiathos Town, is one of the island's hidden gems. With its shallow waters and peaceful atmosphere, it's a perfect spot for families and those looking for a quieter beach experience. The beach is surrounded by green hills and has a small taverna where you can enjoy traditional Greek food. The waters are calm, making it ideal for a relaxing day by the sea without the crowds.

- **Why Visit**: Troulos offers a quiet, relaxing atmosphere and is less crowded than other popular beaches on the island, making it an ideal choice for families and those seeking tranquility.

6. Kastro Village

- **Location**: Northern Skiathos, near the **Kastro Peninsula**
- **Price**: Free
- **Website**: No official website
- **Opening Hours**: Open year-round
- **Key Features**: Historical ruins, breathtaking views, quiet atmosphere

Description:

Kastro, the ancient medieval town of Skiathos, is one of the island's most underrated locations. Perched on a hilltop with views of the sea, Kastro offers a glimpse into the island's past. The site is home to ancient ruins and a small church, with narrow, winding streets and a peaceful atmosphere that makes it perfect for those who want to experience the history and serenity of the island. It's a bit off the beaten path, requiring a short hike from the nearest road, but the journey is well worth it for the stunning views and historical significance.

- **Why Visit**: Kastro is a must-visit for history enthusiasts and those seeking a peaceful, off-the-beaten-path location with incredible panoramic views.

7. Agia Paraskevi Beach

- **Location**: Southern Skiathos, near **Achladies Beach**
- **Price**: Free
- **Website**: No official website
- **Opening Hours**: Open year-round
- **Key Features**: Quiet beach, beautiful surroundings, clear water

Description:

Agia Paraskevi Beach is another lesser-known beach that provides a peaceful retreat from the more popular tourist spots on the island. The beach has golden sand and clear, shallow water, perfect for swimming and relaxing in a calm environment. Surrounded by green hills and small tavernas, the beach offers a serene atmosphere for those looking to unwind away from the crowds.

- **Why Visit**: For its secluded and tranquil vibe, Agia Paraskevi is ideal for travelers who prefer peace and quiet, making it a great escape from the hustle and bustle of more famous beaches.

8. Skiathos Observatory

- **Location**: Near **Skiathos Town**, at the top of a hill
- **Price**: Free
- **Website**: No official website
- **Opening Hours**: Best during the evening, especially during clear nights
- **Key Features**: Stunning views, stargazing, peaceful ambiance

Description:

For those interested in stargazing or simply enjoying a quiet, panoramic view of the island at night, the **Skiathos Observatory** is an underrated spot that offers a calm and serene environment. Located at the top of a hill, this small observatory is the perfect place to unwind and gaze at the stars. It offers spectacular views of the island and the sea, and on clear nights, you can marvel at the night sky.

- **Why Visit**: A perfect spot for a peaceful evening, stargazing, or simply enjoying the tranquility of Skiathos after dark.

Skiathos is a beautiful island with more to offer than just its well-known beaches and bustling town. These local recommendations—whether they be quiet beaches, panoramic viewpoints, or historical sites—give visitors the opportunity to discover a more intimate and peaceful side of the island. By venturing off the beaten path, you'll find hidden gems that allow you to experience the authentic beauty and serenity of Skiathos, making your trip even more special and memorable.

11.3 Travel Hacks for Skiathos

Skiathos is a beautiful island, and while it offers a laid-back atmosphere, there are still ways to enhance your trip with a few travel hacks. These tips and tricks will help you save time, money, and make your vacation more enjoyable while exploring the hidden gems of the island.

1. Rent a Scooter or ATV for Flexible Exploration

- **Hack**: Public transportation can be a bit sparse, and taxis can become expensive. Renting a **scooter or ATV** gives you the freedom to explore Skiathos at your own pace, reaching more secluded beaches, hidden villages, and scenic spots.
- **Tip**: Many rental shops offer discounts for longer rentals (weekly rates are often cheaper). Make sure to book in advance during the peak season to secure the best prices.
- **Benefit**: Flexibility to explore remote locations that are otherwise hard to access.

2. Take Advantage of Early Morning or Late Afternoon Beach Time

- **Hack**: Skiathos can get quite busy, especially in the summer months. To avoid the crowds, head to the beaches early in the morning or later in the afternoon. The best time for a swim or to grab a spot on the sand is either at sunrise or just before sunset when the beaches are much quieter.
- **Tip**: If you're planning on visiting popular beaches like **Koukounaries** or **Banana Beach**, arriving early ensures you can find a good spot and enjoy the clear waters before the crowds gather.
- **Benefit**: Peaceful beach experience and better photo opportunities.

3. Use Local Buses to Get Around on a Budget

- **Hack**: Skiathos has an efficient but affordable local bus system that connects most major attractions and beaches. Instead of spending money on taxis or rental cars, take advantage of the buses for a budget-friendly way to travel around.
- **Tip**: Purchase a **multi-ride bus pass** if you're planning to use the bus frequently. It will save you money over individual tickets, especially if you're visiting multiple beaches and attractions.
- **Benefit**: Budget-friendly transportation option and a great way to interact with locals.

4. Visit Skiathos Town on Foot to Discover Hidden Gems

- **Hack**: **Skiathos Town** is full of charming streets, cozy cafes, and hidden boutiques, but it's easy to miss them if you're focused on the main streets. Wander around the side alleys and walk away from the port area to uncover quieter spots and local gems.
- **Tip**: Take time to explore areas like the **Old Port** and **Bourtzi** Peninsula, where you can find peaceful cafes and picturesque viewpoints without the crowds.
- **Benefit**: Discover hidden gems and enjoy a more authentic experience of Skiathos Town.

5. Pack Light but Smart for Island Adventures

- **Hack**: Skiathos is known for its beaches, hiking trails, and active pursuits. When packing, make sure to bring a small **daypack** for your excursions. Include essentials like sunscreen, a hat, a refillable water bottle, a camera, and comfortable shoes for walking or hiking.
- **Tip**: Leave heavy bags at your hotel and only take what you need for the day, especially when exploring remote areas or beaches.
- **Benefit**: Lightweight and practical packing ensures comfort during island adventures.

6. Use the "Secret Beach" Map for Hidden Gems

- **Hack**: While the most popular beaches like **Koukounaries** and **Elia** are stunning, they can get crowded. Look up the "secret beach" maps on local websites or ask locals for directions to secluded beaches like **Mandraki Beach** or **Xanemos Beach**, which are not well-known to tourists.
- **Tip**: Ask the locals for advice on where to find quiet spots; they often know hidden gems that don't show up in guidebooks or online resources.
- **Benefit**: Enjoy more private, serene beach experiences away from the crowds.

7. Use Cash for Small Purchases to Avoid Hidden Fees

- **Hack**: While many establishments on Skiathos accept credit cards, some smaller shops, tavernas, or local markets may add hidden fees or charges when you use your card. Carry cash for small purchases or in local villages to avoid this.
- **Tip**: Withdraw cash from ATMs in **Skiathos Town** to get better exchange rates or use **Euros**, as it's the official currency on the island.
- **Benefit**: Save on hidden fees and support local businesses.

8. Avoid Peak Dining Hours for Better Experiences

- **Hack**: Restaurants and cafes in Skiathos can get packed, especially during peak hours (typically between 8:00 PM to 10:00 PM). To avoid long wait times and crowded spaces, try to eat **earlier or later** than the usual dining rush.
- **Tip**: If you're craving a specific taverna, consider making a reservation ahead of time or opting for a slightly earlier or later sitting.
- **Benefit**: Enjoy a more relaxed dining experience and avoid waiting in line.

9. Take Advantage of Free Activities

- **Hack**: Skiathos offers a wealth of natural beauty and cultural experiences that don't require an entry fee. **Hiking trails**, **beach walks**, and sightseeing in areas like **Kastro** or **Panagia Evangelistria Monastery** are free and offer a deeper connection with the island's history and landscape.
- **Tip**: Don't miss out on the **Walking Trails of Skiathos**; the island has some beautiful paths that lead to spectacular viewpoints and beaches.
- **Benefit**: Free and enriching activities that let you explore the island in an authentic, budget-friendly way.

10. Book Island Hopping Tours in Advance for the Best Deals

- **Hack**: **Island hopping** is a great way to explore the nearby islands, but prices can vary greatly depending on the time of year and availability. For the best deals, book your boat trips or tours in advance, especially during the busy summer season.
- **Tip**: Many tour operators offer discounts for early bookings or for groups, so it's worth planning ahead if you want to visit nearby islands like **Skopelos** or **Alonissos**.
- **Benefit**: Secure the best deals and avoid last-minute disappointments during peak season.

11. Bring an Extra Power Bank for Your Devices

- **Hack**: Skiathos, especially in more remote areas, may have limited access to charging stations, and you'll likely want to take lots of photos and videos. Bring a portable **power bank** to keep your phone or camera charged throughout the day.
- **Tip**: If you're heading to remote beaches or hiking, make sure your phone is fully charged in case of emergencies.

- **Benefit**: Stay connected, have your devices ready for photos, and ensure you're never left without battery in case you need to contact your accommodation or a tour guide.

By utilizing these travel hacks, you can enhance your experience on Skiathos, save time, avoid unnecessary costs, and enjoy a more relaxed and authentic visit. From hidden beaches to local bus tips, these hacks will help you get the most out of your island getaway while making your trip as smooth and enjoyable as possible.

Printed in Dunstable, United Kingdom

63753686R00092